Ruth the Scroll of Kindness

מגילת רות

Megillas Ruth

with the Commentary Nachalas Yosef
Elucidated by the Insights of Our Sages

by Rabbi Yosef Ze'ev Lipowitz

Translated by Rabbi Yaakov Yosef Iskowitz

FELDHEIM PUBLISHERS
JERUSALEM   NEW YORK

Originally published in 1959 in Hebrew as
Megillas Ruth im Perush Nachalas Yosef.

ISBN 1-58330-484-3

English edition: First published 2001

FELDHEIM PUBLISHERS
POB 35002 / Jerusalem, Israel

202 Airport Executive Park
Nanuet, NY 10954

www.feldheim.com

Printed in Israel

Contents

Foreword

I was happy to hear about the upcoming publication of a new edition of the important book *Nachalas Yosef* on *Megillas Ruth*, written by the distinguished Rabbi Yosef Ze'ev Halevi Lipowitz, *zt"l*.

The reader will find that this is one of our best contemporary books. In addition to explaining the Biblical text in an incisive fashion, according to the words of *Chazal*, it imparts to anyone who studies it ways to conduct oneself, an outlook on life, and good traits.

"Though the wine belongs to the owner, the thanks are given to the butler" — Accolades to the publisher for producing such an up-to-date edition, which will surely be enjoyed by many in our generation.

CB   CB   CB

I knew the author, *zt"l*, for many years. He was unique... distinguished in the way he lived, in his way of thinking, and in his method of disseminating Torah and the fear of Heaven.

During his last years, he was confined to his home due to illness. In his agony he was barely able to read his beloved texts, such as the *Pesikta* or *Seforno*, with a magnifying glass. He painstakingly joined one letter to another, proceeding from verse to verse in the text. It actually rejuvenated him: "Wisdom gives life to him who owns it." Anyone who visited him received a friendly, hearty welcome, and found him full of zeal and joie de vivre. He would read, face life and death, and sing praises.

It was remarkable how his spirit prevailed, how he remained invigorated, ascending to higher levels of delving into the words of our Sages, of the philosophy of life, of noble-mindedness and refinement of character. Even those who had long known him as a source of fertile ideas and a great innovator in the realm of piety, and as one who had a uniquely charming way of expressing himself, were surprised by his ability to process and consolidate these thoughts into all-encompassing philosophy. He did this by paying attention to very fine distinctions in linguistic nuances, and by probing into the depths of the subjects' souls, all with gracious humility, as a good friend, even as a student imbibing knowledge. His erudition flowed freely from his heart to his lips.

He was rooted in a previous generation, as a student of the pious *Ge'onim*, Rabbi Nasan Tzvi Finkel and Rabbi Samson Raphael Hirsch (the latter through his writings), drawing from the wellsprings of Kotzker *Chassidus* on his father's side, and from the great world of Torah and reverence that he embraced. Yet he lived with the troubles of this generation, working diligently and succeeding in finding solutions for them in the Torah and in the plain but penetrating words of our Sages. He strengthened many and brought many to repentance.

Anyone who studies his book on *Megillas Ruth*, which consists of only a small part of his labor, will experience the above.

C3   C3   C3

Dear, delightful R' Yosef Ze'ev! Beloved of Hashem and His people! How he rejoiced upon hearing good tidings concerning the public or an individual, and how he shared in their sorrow! He literally cried for them. His instructive words lifted the stumbling. Routine, worn-out phrases of consolation took on a new and refreshing meaning when uttered by him. How attuned he was to what was going on in the wide world — God's world that strives for redemption after the sin! And how much more so when it came to the world of Judaism, and, especially, the Holy Land that he loved so much. He had a particular love for Torah institutions and scholars — "Adino the Etzni." He illuminated it all with the innovative application of teachings of morality through a comprehensive perspective.

Although he was immersed in the *Aggadeta*, or, more accurately, in the Holy Writings, their *Targumim* and commentaries, it was also a joy to discuss Halachah with him. His proficiency in Torah is attested in his book *Nachalas Yosef* on Talmudic themes, which contains many new interpretations. It is for good reason that many people of various circles felt orphaned by his passing, as, it seems, did books and essays as well. Ink in pens turned into heart's blood — as is that in which these lines, too, are written.

May this new edition of *Nachalas Yosef* enlighten many and serve to elevate the soul of its distinguished author, of blessed memory.

Rabbi Ephraim N. Borodiansky
Former Editor, *The Talmudic Encyclopedia*
12 Elul 5749

This Foreword appeared in the third Hebrew edition of Nachalas Yosef.

Preface

The commentary *Nachalas Yosef* on *Megillas Ruth* was first printed during the lifetime of its author, *zt"l*, in 5719 (1959), and again, after his death, in 5737. Both editions were published by Rabbi Avraham Zioni, *zt"l* (d. 9 Teves 5748).

Those editions were very well received by the reading public and were snatched up very quickly. This soon led to the publication of a third edition. Sadly, just after it had been printed, the Torah world suffered the passing of the great *Ga'on*, Rabbi Ephraim Nachum Borodiansky, *zt"l*, on 26 Shevat 5750. He was a great scholar who was extraordinary in his love of Torah and in his regard for fellow human beings. Rabbi Borodiansky held the author as dear as himself: He highly respected him, often visited him, drank in his Torah and wisdom, and did much to publicize his books and teachings. He contributed his advice, encouragement, and blessings to the present work. May his soul be bound up in the bonds of eternal life.

ɑ ɑ ɑ

Nachalas Yosef has distinguished itself in the following ways:

It is a broad commentary written in a well-polished style on the verses of *Megillas Ruth*, based on the explanations of our Sages and eminent commentators. The personalities and events described therein are illuminated by new insights that are incisive yet clear.

The author presents sources and proofs from the words of *Chazal*. His delving into their words and the pearls he finds therein bring us closer to their world, to their reverence for each letter and crownlet contained in the Biblical verses, and to their incomparable understanding of the spiritual powers of man.

9

Rabbi Lipowitz, *zt"l*, explains the *Megillah* in contemporary terms. He cleverly turned his commentary into a guide on how to acquire good traits, beliefs, and a Torah-true outlook. From his words one may draw plenty of practical ideas that shed true light on our way of life and on many current events. The author succeeded in fashioning a vessel from which many in our generation may quench their thirst. This appears to be one of the few commentaries that teaches us not only the meaning of the text, but also the pragmatic lessons and guidance that can be derived therefrom.

ଓଃ   ଓଃ   ଓଃ

We are indebted to the prominent Torah scholars who guided us in our labor, especially to the great *Ga'on* Rabbi Ephraim Borodiansky, *zt"l*, past editor of the *Talmudic Encyclopedia*, who was very close to the author, *zt"l*. He encouraged us to undertake this sacred task, and it is from him that we heard of the greatness of the author, who had been "like one of the earlier Aggadic rabbis [i.e., homilists]" (as is inscribed on Rabbi Lipowitz's tombstone).

We pray to the One Who dwells on high that the book's contents raise its readers to the spiritual level of *Megillas Ruth*, which is "wholly kindness," in the words of our Sages.

Author's Introduction

I thank Hashem for His kindness to me, and for enabling me to publish comments and elucidations concerning the words of our Sages and early commentators on *Megillas Ruth*. I hope that with God's help these words will assist whoever studies them to derive pleasure from the light of the ancients.

೮೮   ೮೮   ೮೮

The Torah exhorts us to exert ourselves daily in the words of Torah, to revitalize them and not allow them to become obsolete. We see this from the Sages' comment in *Sifri* on the verse, "These things that I am commanding you today shall be [impressed] upon your heart" (*Devarim* 6:6): "Let them not seem to you like an old decree that nobody minds, but like a new one to which everyone runs."

From the *Sifri*'s comment one may derive that if we do not try to renew the words of the Torah daily, they will become obsolete and lose their value and flavor. This charge and warning is repeated in several passages in the Torah. *Chazal* have also said, "They shall appear to you as new every day," applying it to the verse, "You will constantly heed [My commandments]" (*Devarim* 11:13; see *Sifri* and Rashi there), as well as to other passages.

We even find Chazal applying the word "rust" to the aging process of the words of Torah (*Sifri Ha'azinu* 2): "Said Rabbi Ya'akov bar Chanina to Rebbi: 'Let's examine [dust off] *halachos* so they don't rust away.'" That is to say, just as rust can eat away and destroy the hardest substances, it can also permeate spiritual matters, unless one scrutinizes [dusts them off] and renews them.

How can we prevent the words of Torah from becoming "rusty"? *Chazal* have taught us (*Sifri* ibid.): "'Like raindrops on plants' [*Devarim* 32:2] — As raindrops fall on grass, and clean, rub, and cause it to expand, so shall you amplify the words of Torah by reviewing it two, three, and four times." In other words, reviewing the Torah over and over is the only way to prevent it from harmful "rust." Each review also augments and refines it, thus giving it a new taste.

Similarly, our Sages said (*Eruvin* 54b): "As often as the child sucks the breast, so does he find milk in it; so it is with the words of Torah. As often as a man studies them, so does he find relish in them."

In light of our Sages' exhortation, I have not attempted, in my commentary on *Megillas Ruth*, to come up with new interpretations, but merely to extract the deeper meanings from their words, and to gain understanding from the early commentaries.

I must point out to all who might find my thesis to be sound, that I owe this method of understanding the words of *Chazal* to my mentor, the great *Ga'on* Rabbi Nasan Tzvi Finkel, *zt"l*, who was known as the *Alter* of Slobodka. It is similar to the story in the *Talmud Yerushalmi* (*Shekalim* 2:5), where Rabbi Yochanan was annoyed that Rabbi Elazar did not report a certain statement in his name. Rabbi Ya'akov bar Idi appeased him by saying: "Everyone knows that when Rabbi Elazar sits and delivers his discourse, it is your teaching!"

I pray that my words will be acceptable.

May the following statements serve as an eternal memorial to my dear parents who, with great dedication, toiled and strove to guide me in the pursuit of Torah:

My honored father and teacher, Rabbi Baruch ben Yeshayah Elimelech Halevi, *zt"l*, and my modest mother and teacher, Mrs. Liba Etel Bas Avraham (may she rest in Paradise), who are buried in the Holy Land, in Tel Aviv. May their memory be blessed forever.

May the memory of my younger brother, Avraham Meir, *z"l*, also be eternalized, for he died in the prime of life.

May their souls be bound up in the bond of life!

റ്റ   റ്റ   റ്റ

I will give them a monument and a name in My house and within My walls, which is better than sons and daughters. I will give them an eternal name that will never be terminated.
(YESHAYAHU 56:5)

Rabbi Tanchum said: "Bar Kappara expounded in Tzippori, 'This alludes to the Book of Daniel, which was named after him.'"
(SANHEDRIN 93b)

I thank Hashem for enabling me to be among those who sit in the house of study, and Who has granted me the privilege of publishing this commentary on *Megillas Ruth*. I am also grateful to "the one who dwells within the home [and] apportions the booty" (*Tehillim* 65:13): my dear modest wife, whose goodness of heart and hard work enabled me to accomplish it. "May she be blessed more than [the other] women [who dwelled] in tents" (*Shofetim* 5:24): Mrs. Baila (may she live long!) [*z"l*], daughter of the revered Rabbi Nachman, *zt"l*, and his modest wife, Mrs. Shaina Sarah, *z"l*, my father- and mother-in-law. May their memory be blessed forever.

Why Megillas Ruth Is Read on Shavuos

THE VIRTUE OF
PRIVATION AND SUFFERING

What is the connection between Ruth and Shavuos ([the festival of] assembly)? That it is read in an assembly at the time of the giving of the Torah, to teach that the Torah was given through suffering and privation.

(YALKUT RUTH 594)

Shemuel wrote his Book, and Shofetim and Ruth.

(BAVA BASRA 14b)

"A Book of Suffering"

Our Sages called *Megillas Ruth* "A Book of Suffering," as they did the *Book of Iyov*, because both tell about many tragedies that befell distinguished and wealthy families. Upon perusal, we will see that the Megillah comprises all types of human tragedy: those that have to do with the life of the nation, the family, and the individual. There is, however, a great difference between the impression with which each Book — *Iyov* and *Ruth* — leaves us. The passages of *Iyov* infuse us with a spirit of sorrow and gloom, whereas the *Book of Ruth* — although one reads in it about famine, exile, death, and poverty — does not make the reader feel the sadness and sighing therein. This shows us that the intent of the *Book of Iyov* is to stress the full extent of the suffering and sorrow, while the *Book of Ruth* integrates the sufferings not for their own sake, but for their outcome; their end covers over their beginning. So said our Sages regarding the nature of the *Book of Ruth*: "It is a suffering with a sequel [of happiness], as

15

Rabbi Yochanan said: 'Why was she called Ruth [רות]? —
Because David was descended from her, who satiated [רוה] the
Holy One, blessed is He, with hymns and praises' " (*Bava Basra*
14b).

Suffering with a Sequel

It would appear that also the suffering of Iyov has a happy
ending, as it is stated: "The Eternal blessed Iyov's end more than
his beginning" (*Iyov* 42:12). The comparison, however, is only
imaginary. Iyov's end does not evolve from the suffering that
preceded it; it is as though they are two separate things. One
observes the tribulations that came upon a man suddenly, and
that disappeared in like manner. One does not see, however,
that these sufferings yielded him any benefit that would have
made them worthwhile. It may be compared to a horizon
covered by dark clouds, clouds of fury, which later clears up to
show a radiant sun, without having received any rain to quench
the field's thirst. The clouds in the *Book of Ruth*, however,
discharged the beneficial rain that caused the wondrous shoot
called David to grow. This is what the Gemara meant in quoting
Rabbi Yochanan: "Why was she called Ruth [רות]? Because
David was descended from her ...." One might say that Rabbi
Yochanan need not tell us that David descended from Ruth,
because the Megillah itself states that she was the foremother of
the House of David. However, Rabbi Yochanan's insight is that
there is an inner connection between David and Ruth, and that
the satiation that is found in David's hymns had their source in
Ruth.

The Blessing that Comes from Suffering and Privation

What caused Ruth to merit having a descendant comparable
to herself? Her suffering and privation. She was not motivated
to proclaim "Your people is my people, and your God is my
God" during her ten years of bliss in Naomi's family. All her
spiritual advances were made only following her soul's purification in the crucible of suffering and sorrow.

Moreover, her soul had already been anticipated seven
hundred years previously, as hinted at in the verse "And your

two daughters who are [found] here" (*Bereshis* 19:15), concerning which it is written in *Yalkut Shimoni* (84): "[This refers to] the two finds — Ruth the Moabite and Na'amah the Ammonite." Should we not have expected that Ruth's clinging to the Jewish people would come through happiness and plenty? In spite of that, the remarkable chain of events came about through suffering and privation.

In the very same way, through sadness and suffering, Naomi too returned to her people and her country, meriting that through her the monarchy of the House of David would be built. Every sprouting and growth requires rain, but the power of rain is potent only when the planting takes place in the bosom of the earth. Similarly, suffering is effective only with him in whose heart lies a good seed. That is why the suffering did not affect Machlon and Kilyon. It did, however, influence Naomi, and especially Ruth, who was privileged to become the mother of royalty and of the Mashiach [may he come speedily in our time, Amen].

Consolation for Yisrael's Suffering

The story of Ruth also gives solace to the suffering and hardship of the entire Jewish people. The Torah is one of three gifts God presented to the Jews through suffering. The many tribulations of the Jewish people are connected to the giving of the Torah, for when that happened "eternal hatred for the eternal nation" was born, as explained by our Sages (see Rashi, *Eichah* 1:21). It was on Shavuos, the time of the giving of the Torah, that Chazal chose to make the Jewish people aware of the value of suffering and the blessing hidden therein. This is also alluded to in the aforementioned words of the *Yalkut*: "What is the connection between Ruth and Shavuos ([the festival of] assembly)? That it is read in an assembly at the time of the giving of the Torah, to teach that the Torah was given through suffering and privation."

On Shavuos, Megillas Ruth was given to us as a consolation. The Megillah teaches us that the greatest accomplishments sprout from suffering and oppression. It is worth every Jew's while to examine the story of the Megillah and Ruth's way of life in order to learn from her fate about the good end that awaits the Jewish people in the days to come.

THE VIRTUE OF KINDNESS

Why is this Megillah read on the Festival of Shavuos?
Because this Megillah is wholly kindness, and the Torah is
full of kindness, as it is written: 'And the teaching [lit.,
Torah] of kindness was on her tongue' [Mishlei 31:26], and
it was given on Shavuos.

(MIDRASH LEKACH TOV)

In addition to the teaching about suffering, the Sages emphasized the lesson to be learned from the kindness in *Megillas Ruth*:
"Said Rabbi Ze'ira, 'This Megillah contains neither impurity nor
purity [laws], nor [laws about] what is forbidden and what is
permissible. Why, then, was it written? To teach how great is the
reward of those who perform kindnesses' " (*Ruth Rabbah* 2:15).

Justice, Righteousness, and Kindness

In his *Moreh Nevuchim* (3:53), the Rambam analyzes the true
nature of the term "kindness" (חסד). He explains how kindness
differs from justice and righteousness. Justice refers to any
payment of a debt, in accordance with the law. Righteousness
(צדקה), however, which is itself derived from justice (צדק), is not
an obligation mandated by common law, but rather something
that one feels motivated on his own to perform, as the Rambam
states: "When one fulfills those duties towards others because of
one's moral conscience...for when one acts virtuously, one acts
justly towards one's intellectual faculty." Kindness, on the other
hand, is completely beyond any feelings of obligation, as the
Rambam writes: "In Scripture, most of the references to חסד
connote bestowing kindness upon someone to whom one has no
obligation at all."

"The World Is Built on Kindness"

The creation of the world was a supreme deed of kindness.
It contained not an element of obligation to anyone; rather, it
was totally an act of goodness. As Chazal explain: "The world
was created solely to enjoy God and to bask in the glory of the
Divine Presence." The design of Creation is the benefit of its

creatures themselves, and that is kindness in its purest sense, as it is written: "The world is built on kindness" (*Tehillim* 89:3) — The building of the world is kindness.

Human beings, who are created in the image of God, can and must attain the spiritual level of kindness. Kindness is the standard by which man may be measured; it reveals his degree of spirituality. It is through kindness that man may rise above egotism, a thing that is inherent in all creatures, because they all have a tendency toward self-preservation. Man, too, is imbued with self-centeredness; he is no different from other creatures when doing things that benefit himself. One's ability to act freely, motivated by a pure spiritual source, can only be revealed through deeds of kindness, performed altruistically and without the demands of external or internal laws.

Since man's senses do not contain a source for such a characteristic, the source must lie in man's Creator, on the basis of, "He Who implants the ear, does He not hear? He Who forms the eye, does He not see?" (*Tehillim* 94:9). From this we may conclude that in every manifestation of the attribute of kindness lies proof to the beginning of Creation. And just as the Creator began creating His world before there was any law that demanded it, so is man, too — when he performs an act of kindness without any force impelling him to do so — beginning from that point of Creation when he was likened to his Creator and the image of God in him shone in all its brilliance.

Kindness and the World's Existence

In the same way as the creation of the world was an act of kindness, so is ongoing kindness necessary for the world's continued existence, as alluded to in Eisan ha-Ezrachi's words, "I will sing forever about the kindness of the Eternal" (*Tehillim* 89:2). Our Sages elaborate on that passage: "They asked Eisan, 'On what does the world stand?' and he answered, 'On kindness,' as it is stated: The throne will be established with kindness" (*Yeshayahu* 16:5). This may be compared to a chair that had four legs, one of which was wobbly, so that it took a chip to steady it. So had the throne of the Holy One, blessed is He, been tottering, so to speak, until He steadied it. And with what? With kindness. Consequently, "I said, The world is built on kindness" (*Yalkut Tehillim*). Accordingly, it is God's kindness that gives the world its stability. Indeed, one of His titles is "Abundant in Kindness" (*Shemos* 34:6, The Thirteen Attributes of Mercy).

Neither can man's own world exist without a foundation of kindness, as attested by Shimon ha-Tzaddik's statement that deeds of kindness are one of the three pillars upon which the world stands (*Avos* 1:2). And just as the work of Creation is, as it were, not yet complete — as Chazal alluded to in their statement that "one of the earth's flanks has remained exposed" (*Pirkei d'Rabbi Eliezer*) — enabling all types of calamities to befall it and its inhabitants, so is our human world incomplete and defective. Man is endowed with the ability to perfect himself and the entire world, and to become a partner of God in building His world. This action constitutes kindness, and it is in its performance that man fulfills his share in "The world is built on kindness." Kindness is the basis for the perfection of the world and the cornerstone for the Messianic days. It is the glue that will link all humanity and make it into one fraternity. Every assurance uttered by the prophets, and every promise they ever made — concerning societal as well as individual peace, down to "I will eliminate wild beast from the land" (*Vayikra* 26:6) — is based on kindness.

"And What the Eternal Requires of You..."

A purpose of prophecy was to rid us of the notion that there are alternative ways to achieve goodness. The Prophet Michah says: "[The Eternal] has informed you, man, what is good [for you to do] and what the Eternal requires of you. [It is] just to carry out justice and acts of lovingkindness, and to follow [the ways of] your God modestly" (*Michah* 6:8). Everything a man is drawn toward because it appears to be good is only deceptively so. Genuine good — that which God requires of man — begins with justice and rises and ascends to acts of lovingkindness, which is the highest level of goodness.

This concept is expanded upon in the words of the Prophet Yirmeyahu: "This is what the Eternal has said: 'Let not the wise man praise himself for his wisdom, the mighty man praise himself for his strength, or the rich man praise himself for his wealth. However, he who praises himself may praise himself for this: [for] acting intelligently and recognizing [My ways], for I am the Eternal Who does kindness, justice, and righteousness on earth, because it is these [attributes] which I desire. [This is] the prophetic declaration of the Eternal' " (*Yirmeyahu* 9:22–23). Obviously, this cannot be referring to self-praise, for "he who praises himself may praise himself for this" would contradict the fact that one must not claim merit for one's Torah and good deeds, since they are one's raison d'etre. This is even more so regarding one's God-given talents. Rather, these verses answer the question, "What are the values that make life worthwhile?" Some may consider wisdom per se to be life's paramount value, while others may substitute the manifestation of man's strength and power. Others yet may emphasize a life of plenty and happiness. The prophet, however, establishes that even someone as wise as Shelomo, as strong as Shimshon, or as rich as Korach (see Targum), cannot praise himself as having discovered man's objective and purpose in the world.

The prophet's words obviously also neutralize the cultural developments of our generation, which have added to our knowledge and given man control over the forces of nature, thus improving man's living conditions and increasing his material wealth to the point where he now possesses wisdom, power, and wealth simultaneously. Clearly, all these have not brought man happiness, but merely its semblance. The Angel of Death and all other evil angels accompany them, for they lack a foundation of kindness. All the wise, powerful, and wealthy, who are in control of the achievements of modern culture, are constrained to the world's destruction, not to its progression. Therefore, wisdom, power, and wealth, which are not impelled by the spirit of kindness, are detrimental to man, and are not the goal of creation.

What God desires of His creatures is kindness, justice, and righteousness, and, as we have seen, the latter two are incomplete without the former. Only when justice and righteousness are combined with kindness, do wisdom, power, and wealth have value. Until then, they are as a body without a soul. Then, and only then, "he who praises himself may praise himself" through all of them.

Kindness — The Root of All Good Attributes

When Eliezer went to take a wife for Yitzchak, from whom the House of Yisrael would be built, he tested her neither in wisdom nor other virtues, but through an act of kindness — providing water for man and beast. This small act outweighs even the wonderful inventions of man's mind, because it creates a point from which all man's deeds may germinate, serving as the seed which will eventually sprout the redemption of the world.

The great virtue of an act of kindness may also be seen in Moshe's name. Our Sages, in the Gemara (*Megillah* 13a) and in the Midrash (*Vayikra Rabbah* 1:3), list the ten names of Moshe, showing how each described one of his attributes — for example, "Yered [ירד], for he caused the Shechinah to descend [הוריד]...Chever [חבר], because he joined [חיבר] the children [of Yisrael] to their Father in heaven." Bisyah, Paroh's daughter, called him Moshe [משה], to point out that she had pulled him [משתה] out of the water. It was precisely this name that remained in the Torah, though it does not express any of Moshe's greatness, as our Sages commented: "She named him Moshe — From this one may learn how great is the reward of those who perform kindnesses. Although Moshe had many names, the only one used in the Torah is that given to him by Bisyah, the daughter of Paroh. Even the Holy One, blessed is He, did not call him by any other name" (*Shemos Rabbah* 1:31). We see that the name of Moshe — who brought down the Torah from heaven — served only to commemorate an act of kindness, to memorialize Bisyah who saved Moshe.

Kindness is the basis of the entire Torah. It is also the basis of Megillas Ruth, as Chazal stated in *Midrash Lekach Tov*: "Why is this Megillah read on the festival of Shavuos? It is because this Megillah is wholly kindness, and the Torah is completely kindness, as it is written: 'And the teaching of kindness was on her tongue' [*Mishlei* 31:26], and it was given on Shavuos."

"This Megillah Is Wholly Kindness"

The attestation given by the Jewish people through reading the Megillah on the Festival of Shavuos has no parallel in any other nation. No other people would reveal and publicize the lowly origins of its royal house. The Jewish people proclaim on the festival of the giving of the Torah that the House of David, to which eternal reign had been promised, was descended from a contemptible nation, with whom the Torah forbids intermarriage. Furthermore, it is emphasized that a stain had been found among the nobility of Yehudah, destined to become Yisrael's royalty, whereas a foreign young woman had been found to be better and more worthy than they, so that it was her descendants who received the crown of royalty in perpetuity. Seemingly, we should be ashamed to read this story that removes the royal attire from Yisrael's great and noble ones and places it upon a Mo'aviyah convert. It is a fact, however, and the prophet saw the need to write a special book about it and to tell it in detail. Why? To make it known that there is such a thing as kindness in the world, and that all the world's hope hinges on it. The Megillah teaches us that Ruth's following an old, lonely woman to an unfamiliar country, sharing her lot in silent support, is the kindness of which it is said, "It is these [attributes] which I desire" (*Yirmeyahu* 9:23).

Kindness passes as a gossamer thread through both parts of the Megillah — that of the descent as well as that of the ascent, the tribulations and the happy ending. Its fallen as well as its exalted people are focused around this principle. The prophet uses both as examples. On the one hand, he shows us how selfishness and the lack of kindness causes even the greatest of the greats to lose everything. Conversely, we see the results of kindness, in that even the lowliest merits every good thing because of its practice.

The scope of the Megillah is much broader than merely encompassing the idea of reward to those who perform kind acts and punishment to those who withhold them. As will be explained, according to the words of Chazal, the downfall of that whole era was due to the absence of kindness; that is, everyone's egoism took priority over the needs of others. This led to "everyone did what was right in his eyes," and to the "judging of the Judges." It led eventually to the departure of Elimelech and his family from the land, and to all the ensuing threats to the existence of the Jewish people. And where did salvation come from? From the wellsprings of kindness that Ruth brought with her, and from her like counterpart in Yisrael, Bo'az. From the re-establishment of the root of kindness in Yisrael, the nation was healed, and from that root all mankind's redemption would sprout.

There are many small deeds of kindness in the Megillah, through which is woven a thread of kindness. The prophet, author of the Megillah, teaches us that in order to save a people from its decline, and to put it back on track, it is not necessary to perform earthshaking things, but rather small acts between man and his fellow. This will lead to the formation of a new being. The future of the world is built on the affinity and relations of kindness between people. No other principle has the power to correct mankind and to extricate it from its troubles, except kindness, for it is the basis of the beginning of Creation and its final goal. Every step in that direction brings the ship of humanity closer to shore. Megillas Ruth presents us with the ultimate objective and shows us the way toward it. It comes to instill within us the realization that little deeds are the way to the kingdom of Mashiach. This is what the Megillah is all about, as well as its lesson for all generations.

"THE LAND WILL BE FILLED ...
JUST AS THE WATER COVERS THE SEA"

It also behooves us to look at the Megillah's style and strategy. The book does not describe a life of opulence, outer glory, or splendor. Similarly, it contains nothing that would really irritate the reader. Everything is described simply and humbly, calmly and patiently. Even the grim situations of famine, exile, death, poverty, and fear — as well as moments of spiritual courage, of overcoming all one's instincts, and of all forms of self-sacrifice — are presented without fanfare, complaint, or praise; in other words, with no "sound of triumph or of defeat." Indeed, the entire book has an aura of calmness, as a tranquil sea.

The prophets compared the gentile world to the sea: "Woe to the roar of many nations, who roar as the roar of the seas" (*Yeshayahu* 17:12). "But the wicked are like the driven sea, which cannot rest..." (ibid. 57:20). Let us examine this analogy. A turbulent sea tosses water from one place to another with a roar and a tremor, ebbing here and swelling there, repeating the cycle over and over, as a sick person who finds no rest. Its loud and tumultuous waves merely reflect the sea in its state of agitation; perhaps they are only its sighs and groans, but do not epitomize its essence, when it is at rest. The remarkable tranquillity of the sea, whose vast waters were gathered together by the design of the Creator, is really its natural look. All its waves and surges are just passing phenomena that appear because of winds and other external factors.

It is to these waves that the prophets compared the gentile world, when its nations erupt and arise against one another and are all in a state of unrest. These tumultuous periods arise out of mankind's malady; it is what causes all the turmoil and rage. A day will come, however, when the sickness will be healed and the waves will be stilled. Mankind will calm down and be like the great sea in the time of its tranquillity, when the reign of the many waters will spread from one edge of the heavens to the other, and there will be none to make them afraid. Perhaps that is what is meant by: "A [royal] staff will then be produced from the family line of Yishai...for the land will be filled with [those who seek] to know the Eternal, just as the water covers the sea" (*Yeshayahu* 11:1-9).

That is the style and character of the Book of Ruth, which tells of a family that lay the foundation for a reconstructed world, planting in it forbearance and serenity, which all mankind will enjoy at the time of the Redemption.

The Era of the Judges

BASED ON THE INTRODUCTION TO
MEGILLAS RUTH IN MIDRASH RABBAH

"The Days When the Judges Governed"

The Megillah does not mention precisely when the events therein took place; rather, it states broadly, "in the days when the Judges governed," which includes a period of nearly four hundred years. This implies that these events are rooted in that entire era and evolve from it. That is why the Sages of the Midrash dedicated almost all their forewords to our Megillah to explaining the features of the Era of the Judges; without this background we would be unable to plunge into the depths of Megillas Ruth.

We know from the Scriptures, as well as from the words of Chazal in many places, that the Era of the Judges exemplified a great decline in the spiritual, moral, and social life of the Jewish people (it was typified by idolatry, the concubine of Givah, and "everyone doing what was right in his eyes"). Our Sages wrote about the character of that generation: "What generation was totally vain? You must say, the generation when the judges governed [lit., 'of the judging of the Judges,' that is, when people judged their Judges!]" (*Bava Basra* 15b).

This decline came soon after the death of Yehoshua, as it is written: "The people served the Eternal all the days of Yehoshua and all the days of the elders who prolonged their days after Yehoshua" (*Shofetim* 2:7). Chazal infer: "They prolonged 'their days,' but not years" (*Shabbos* 105b). The situation changed rapidly, as Scripture attests: "Another generation arose after them that did not know the Eternal, nor the deeds that He had

26

performed for Yisrael. And the Children of Yisrael did what was evil in the eyes of the Eternal, and worshipped the Ba'alim" (*Shofetim* 2:10–11).

The Spiritual Decline
Derived from a Pursuit of the Material

What caused the rapid and terrible decline after the generation of Moshe and Yehoshua? What illness penetrated the Jewish people and eroded its spirit and soul? Clearly, this degeneration did not occur suddenly, but developed in stages, as does a physical illness that appears in one part of the body and spreads until it consumes the entire body. Scripture only records the generation's total corruption, with no hint as to what caused it.

Chazal, however, through their Divine inspiration, did reveal to us the origin of the malady that yielded such negative consequences in the Era of the Judges. It is told concerning the death of Yehoshua: "Yehoshua Bin Nun, the servant of the Eternal, died...and they buried him...north of Mount Ga'ash" (*Yehoshua* 24:29–30; *Shofetim* 2:8–9). Death and burial, and no more. In the Heavenly description of the verses of Scripture there is no sign of mourning over Yehoshua, nor mention of his having been eulogized. "Yisrael showed laxity by not performing a kindness toward Yehoshua" (see *Shabbos* 105b and *Yalkut Shimoni Yehoshua* 35).

The above passages contain an allusion to the explanation of this perplexing issue. "Ga'ash" here refers not to a place; it rather describes the state of the nation. This is how our Sages explain the nation's condition at the time of Yehoshua's burial: "Rabbi Berechiah said: 'We have searched through all of Scripture and have not found mention of a place called Ga'ash [געש — mentioned in reference to Yehoshua's burial; see *Yehoshua* 24:30]. It must be that the text is hinting that the nation was too preoccupied [נתגעשו] to properly honor Yehoshua. It was during the time that the Land of Israel was being divided up, and they had become too engrossed in the division. The people were involved in various tasks: one was busy with his field, and another with his vineyard, etc.' " (foreword to *Ruth Rabbah*, 2).

Their preoccupation [התגעשׁוּתם] with dividing up the land caused them to refrain from performing a kindness for Yehoshua. Though they were carrying out the Torah's command of settling the land ("When you come to the land [of Israel] and [you shall] plant any [kind of] fruit-bearing tree" [*Vayikra* 19:23]), they were not performing it in the spirit of the Torah. Every material endeavor is delimited and bounded in order to prevent it from consuming man's spirit and soul. Our Sages set the proper balance between the physical and the spiritual by stating, "Reduce your business activities and occupy yourself with the Torah instead" (*Avos* 4:10). This rule applies also to activities concerning social welfare or settling the Land of Israel (see quote from *Tanna d'Vei Eliyahu* below).

The people of Yehoshua's generation became so attached to and preoccupied with their estates that they had no inclination or time to bestow a kind deed upon the man who distributed their inheritances. For what is the characteristic of kindness? It is the attribute by which man divests himself, in small or large measure, of selfishness, on behalf of others. He who is immersed in material acquisitions, and is worried about satisfying himself, is incapable of performing acts of kindness.

The Obligation to Teach Torah to the People

Chazal blamed also the leaders of the people and its elders for the generation's decline, as they stated: "Why were 70,000 of Binyamin killed at Givah [see *Shofetim* 19]? Because the Great Sanhedrin left by Moshe, which included Yehoshua and Pinchas ben Elazar, should have girded themselves with steel cords, raised their clothes above their knees, and traveled throughout Israel's cities — one day to Lachish, another to Beis El, and so on — teaching proper behavior to the Jewish people for one, two, even three years, until the people were settled in their land, in order that the Name of the Holy One, blessed is He, become magnified and sanctified in all the worlds He had created. They did not do so, however. Rather, when they entered their land, each came into his own vineyard and field, becoming indifferent to the problems of others, so as to minimize their own inconvenience. Thus the Sages said: 'Reduce your business activities and occupy yourself with the Torah instead' " (*Tanna d'Vei Eliyahu Rabbah* 11).

Here we learn how great is the obligation of the wise men of Yisrael to teach the people Torah and proper behavior in any manner and at all costs, even in a generation whose ears are closed to it. That is why that generation's leaders — who did not fulfill their duty to teach Torah and proper conduct — are blamed. Chazal also attribute to them the severe consequences of the incident regarding the concubine of Givah, which resulted in the killing of 70,000 Jews.

"Laziness Brings on Deep Sleep"

Symptoms of the malady had actually been detected at the time of Yehoshua's death. From then on, the disorder became ever more entrenched in the soul of the nation, to the point where it shattered the House of Yisrael. Our Sages, in an introduction to the Megillah, present before us the whole process of ruination — its beginning, development, and results — based on the verse, "Laziness brings on deep sleep, but the deceptive soul will go hungry" (*Mishlei* 19:15). The text identifies four links that evolve from one another: laziness, deep sleep, a deceptive soul, and hunger. Every one of them appeared during the Era of the Judges, as Chazal explain: "Laziness brings on deep sleep" — Yisrael was lazy about doing kindness to Yehoshua. "The deceptive soul will go hungry" — They deceived the Holy One, blessed is He, some even resorting to idolatry. Hence He withheld (literally, "starved them from") His Divine Spirit, as it is written, "The word of the Eternal was rare in those days" (*Shemuel I* 3:1). Laziness regarding the performance of goodness brought deep sleep onto one's soul, so that people stopped distinguishing between good and evil.

Seemingly, they were diligently immersed in settling the Land of Israel, a mitzvah that is equivalent to and as significant as upholding the Torah. That diligence, however, was tainted with deceit toward God, as the people were really occupied with increasing their own possessions and wealth, straying from the path of the Torah that had admonished them, "Be careful that your hearts do not entice [you]" (*Devarim* 11:16), which Chazal explained as follows: "He said to them, 'Beware of being misled by the evil inclination to forsake the Torah, for he who abandons the Torah becomes attached to idolatry' " (*Sifrei*). This warning had fully materialized in that era: Perhaps they had not felt it at first, but their evil inclination initially caused them to act fraudulently toward God, eventually leading them to the worst treachery of all, idolatry. However, "The deceptive soul will go hungry" (*Mishlei* 19:15): The soul that is overtaken by false things will feel empty and starved. A spiritual famine spread throughout the land, and there was no way to break it because God's word was lacking in that generation, as it is written: "The word of the Eternal was rare in those days" (*Shemuel I* 3:1).

"The Deceptive Soul Will Go Hungry"

The Prophet Amos, too, speaks of this hunger (8:11–12): "Behold, days are coming — [this being] the prophetic declaration of the Lord, Eternal God — when I will send a famine upon the land: not a hunger for bread nor a thirst for water, but for hearing the words of the Eternal. [People] will wander from sea to sea and from north to east to seek the word of the Eternal, but they will not find it." This does not mean, of course, that they will go out to apprehend and seek the word of God, for that would reflect a sublime state, rather than a descent. The prophet must be speaking, however, about a time of spiritual decline, such as our own, when all disdainful slogans have been disproven and all refined philosophies have been found to be false, when one's soul is empty and dry, wandering in every direction in want of something to satisfy its hunger and thirst. For what it is lacking is the word of God, and it cannot find the way to it. That is what happened to that generation of "total vanity," that began with an excessive pursuit after material possessions, a laziness to perform acts of kindness, spiritual slumber, and a deceptive soul, ending up with utter emptiness and starvation.

Falling from Great Heights

This process took place in the beginning of the journey of the Jewish people, soon after the generation of Moshe and

Yehoshua. It therefore constituted a fall from the great heights of the Revelation at Mount Sinai, where the people had said, "We will carry out and heed," to the depths of spiritual degeneration. The possibility of such rapid deterioration is shocking. Chazal wondered about it and interpreted (in paragraph 3 of the Introduction to *Ruth Rabbah*) the following verse as applying to Yisrael and God: "The conduct of man is in constant change, he is a stranger to the right way; but the One of inner purity, His doings are straightforward" (*Mishlei* 21:8). As soon as Yisrael arrived at its state of rest and security, feeling like any nation that dwells in its land, it began exhibiting very strongly that human weakness of fickle-mindedness, or inconsistency, which facilitates rapid backsliding and unobstructed falling from the greatest heights to the lowest depths. Being inconsistent in spirit led to unfaithfulness to their word, as they ignored promises they had made at Sinai. According to Chazal, it was to that generation that the following words of *Ha'azinu* applied: "For they are a generation [that causes] transformation [of My will]; children who have none [of My] upbringing... I said [to Myself], 'I will cast them away as [if] ownerless...' " (*Devarim* 32:20–26).

"My Strength and the Power of My Hand"

That was not the end, however, of the sins of that generation. Continuing their analysis, Chazal detected another weakness, which is discussed in *Ruth Rabbah*. Rabbi Yehudah ben Simon said: "He said, 'Let Me make Myself [as if] oblivious to them' " [*Devarim* 32:20]. This resembles a prince who goes out to the marketplace where he strikes and humiliates others without being hit or humiliated by them. Then he runs over to his father, who says to him, "You think the deference they are showing you is due to your own honor? It is only because of my honor that they respect you." His father then began ignoring him, causing everyone else to pay no attention to the prince as well. This, too, is what happened to the Jewish people: After they had been victorious over great nations, conquering their fortified cities and instilling fear in the hearts of all peoples, they became arrogant and began attributing all their victories to their own power and might. Their ingratitude to Yehoshua led eventually to their being ungrateful toward God. It was as if they attempted to usurp all the credit from God for everything from the exodus from Egypt through the conquest of the land. It is to this that the exhortation in *Ha'azinu* (*Devarim* 32:20) applies: "Let Me make Myself [as if] oblivious to them, [and] see what [kind of] end they have."

As stated above, for various reasons (explained in paragraphs 3 and 4 of the Introduction to *Ruth Rabbah*), these harsh verses were pertinent to the Era of the Judges. Nevertheless, not all of the warranted punishments befell the Jewish people then. Thus *Chazal* explained the verse (*Mishlei* 21:8) as follows: "The conduct of man is in constant change" — this refers to the Jewish people; "but the One of inner purity, His doings are straightforward" — this refers to the Holy One, blessed is He, Who treats them in a straightforward manner. In other words, despite all their inconsistencies, God does not judge them stringently. We may glean what they really deserved from the words of our Sages: "Said the Holy One, blessed is He, 'My children are obstinate; it is impractical to destroy them, to return them to Egypt, or to substitute another nation for them. What shall I therefore do to them? I will bring afflictions upon them and purify them through hunger,' as it is written: It was in the days when the Judges governed [the people] and there was a famine in the land" (*Ruth* 1:1). This means that things had deteriorated to the point where God considered annihilating the Jewish People, or exchanging them for another nation, God forbid, because their behavior no longer justified their existence. It was only due to His having made an eternal covenant with their forefathers that God made an effort to heal their malady through affliction. That is why there was a famine in the days of the Judges. That which to human eyes appeared as adversity and a plague was administered by Divine Providence with benign intentions. Indeed, good and blessings would yet sprout forth from it. The affliction was actually the beginning of the healing process; sorrow and distress were the dew and rain that would cause spiritual growth and flowering.

"Hear, My People, and I Will Speak"

In that era, Yisrael's being worthy of continuing to be called "My people" was weighed on the Heavenly scales and found to be in Yisrael's favor. Therefore, our Sages opened their Introduction to *Midrash Rabbah* on *Ruth* with the verse: "Hear, My people, and I will speak" (*Tehillim* 50:7). The people of Yisrael alone merited being called "My people," an appellation that makes it unique and exalted above all seventy nations, marking it as the nation of God. The whole eternal essence of the Jewish people is embodied in that word.

How and when did the Jewish people attain that designation, one that is unequalled in greatness and importance? The answer, as explained by our Sages, lies in that same verse, "Hear, My people": Rabbi Yudan said, "Formerly, Yisrael was called by its name, as were all other nations. 'By what merit have you deserved to be called My people? By and I will speak — that you spoke before Me in Sinai, saying, We will carry out and heed everything that the Eternal has spoken.' " The title "My people" had not been given to the Jewish people at their inception; nor was it assigned them gratis. Rather, Yisrael raised itself to that lofty level during the Revelation at Mount Sinai. When God "visited" all the nations, offering them the Torah, they asked, "What is written therein?" No nation wished to receive a Torah that places restrictions on man and that seems to constrict his will and freedom. Only the Jewish people did not investigate whether the Torah met its needs; they promised to fulfill the Torah unconditionally, even before learning of its contents. That is why they became God's nation.

The Jewish people, however, did not remain on the spiritual level they had attained at Sinai. They descended to the point where the nations' guardian angels could use the following argument against them: "These [Yisrael] serve idols, and these [the nations] worship idols; these are immoral, and these are immoral; these committed murder, and these committed murder. Why, then, should these ascend to Paradise and these to Gehinnom?" Their argument is apparently so convincing that it silences Michael, the advocate of Yisrael. God, however, says to him: "You have been silenced and cannot speak in the defense of My people? By your life, I will speak righteously and save My children." Yisrael is protected by righteousness even when accusations against it are very strong. Our Sages explain further: "What righteousness? There is a difference of opinion between Rabbi Elazar and Rabbi Yochanan. One of them said that it is the righteousness 'that you performed regarding My world, when you accepted My Torah. For had you not accepted My Torah, I would have returned the world to desolation and nothingness.' The other said that it refers to the righteousness 'you did for yourself by accepting My Torah, for if you had not, I would have wiped you off the face of the earth.' "

This implies that there are two aspects to the Jewish people's receiving the Torah. First, it is to Torah that the world owes its existence, for a world without Torah has no reason or right to exist. Although the world did not acknowledge the Torah or live according to it even after it had been received, since it did after all come down from heaven, it will eventually — following many ordeals, descents and ascents — become absorbed, and perfect the world through the Almighty's sovereignty, in the words of the prophet: "For just as rain and snow come down from heaven and do not return there, but rather they irrigate the earth and make it germinate and grow [vegetation], and they produce seed for him who sows, and food for him who eats, so is My word that comes forth from My mouth — it does not return to Me without effect, but only if it carried out what I desired, and was successful in what I sent it [to do]" (Yeshayahu 55:10–11). Similarly do the other prophets promise in their exhortations, for example, "O Eternal! [You are] my strength, fortitude, and pride on the day of distress. Nations will come to You from the far ends of the earth and say, 'Our fathers inherited [nothing] but falsehood; futile things that have no purpose' " (Yirmeyahu 16:19); or, "For then I will make the nation speak a pure language, so that they all invoke the Eternal by name, to worship Him in unison" (Tzefanyah 3:9). Thus, by the actual receiving of the Torah, the Jewish people saved the world, an act that is to their eternal credit even in times when they themselves stray from its path.

The second aspect is the inner strength the Jewish people revealed when they rose to the spiritual level of receiving the Torah, proclaiming, "We will carry out and heed." This attests to their everlasting ideal, concerning which it is written: "The [Eternal,] Victor of Yisrael, will not lie" (*Shemuel I* 15:29). They are capable of rising following even many falls, as Megillas Ruth demonsrates by showing how afflictions kindled the Godly spark in the Jewish people (see our commentary to *Ruth* 1:6, "...that the Eternal had taken account of His people..."). The purpose of this Introduction (by the Sages to *Ruth Rabbah*) is to prove that there will always be hope for the world through the Jewish people. For just as the Jewish people were the first to accept the Torah and to undertake to observe it, thus setting an example for the whole world as to how exalted man is able to be, so is this people also destined to become an example and a model of how to uphold and actualize it. They therefore have the merit and the righteousness for redemption in any situation, as Scripture implies, "[It is] I, Who speaks of [the forefathers'] righteousness [and has revealed Himself as One Who] has much [power] to save [His people]" (*Yeshayahu* 63:1) — the righteousness of being emissaries and models to the world, as they did when they received the Torah.

We see from all the above that in the Era of the Judges, the Jewish people had been on the verge of destruction, and that as a result of events narrated in the Megillah the people arose from their plunge. Indeed, whereas the Megillah opens with the "fallen mighty ones" (Midrash) of "the days when the Judges governed," it closes with the birth of "Oved, the father of Yishai, the father of David" — the man who solidified the revival of the Jewish nation for generations to come, as we declare: "David, King of Yisrael, is alive and permanent."

Megillas Ruth serves as a prophetic synopsis of the Era of the Judges and as the gateway to the redemption of the Jewish people by the "[royal] staff that will be produced from the family line of Yishai, and the sapling that will sprout from its roots" (*Yeshayahu* 11:1).

מגילת רות

א

(א) וַיְהִי בִּימֵי שְׁפֹט הַשֹּׁפְטִים וַיְהִי רָעָב בָּאָרֶץ וַיֵּלֶךְ אִישׁ מִבֵּית לֶחֶם יְהוּדָה לָגוּר בִּשְׂדֵי מוֹאָב הוּא וְאִשְׁתּוֹ וּשְׁנֵי בָנָיו:

1 (1) *And it was in the days when the Judges governed [the people; lit. "days of the judgment of the Judges"], and there was a famine in the land [of Yisrael], that a [great] man from Beis Lechem [in] Yehudah went to sojourn in the fields of Mo'av — he, with his wife and two sons.*

THREE CALAMITIES

1. And it was in the days when the Judges governed, and there was a famine in the land, that a [great] man from Beis Lechem Yehudah went...

We have already noted that Scripture does not specify exactly when the events of this Megillah occurred. It rather ascribes them to the broad setting of an entire era, that of the Judges, attributing its events to the peculiarities that marked that period. Elimelech's sojourn to Mo'av is not merely a result of the famine; rather, both the famine and Elimelech's trip are consequences of "the days when the Judges governed." Our Sages took pains to explain that the Prophet [Shemuel], who authored this Megillah, does not mention the Era of the Judges incidentally, but does so to reiterate all that had been said in the Book of Judges about that period, pronouncing his judgment upon it in concise prophetic terms.

"And It Was" — An Expression of Trouble

Chazal have a tradition that the scriptural word vayehi (and it was) is used specifically as a reference to the trouble

36

intrinsic to what is being narrated. Thus, they have said in the Gemara and Midrash: "Wherever in the Scripture we find the term *vayehi*, it indicates trouble" (*Megillah* 10b; *Vayikra Rabbah* 11:7). An even stronger expression is *"Vayehi biymei* [And it was in the days of]," which is a harbinger of terrible trouble and danger. Chazal determined that during the entire Biblical period there occurred only five instances of adversity of such magnitude that were distinguished by the expression "Vayehi biymei." Indeed, one of them is: "And it was in the days when the Judges governed." It would appear that the difficult situation alluded to in that expression was connected to the "famine in the land." However, the famine, too, is prefaced by the word "vayehi [and there was]." Therefore, the severe trouble implied at the beginning of the verse must be connected to "the days when the Judges governed [lit. in the days of the judgment of the Judges]," meaning the days when "the people judged the Judges for their evil deeds."

Corruption pervaded all elements of society, flowing from the highest downward, and from the lowest upward: "The generation adapted to its provider, and the provider conformed to his generation." A situation arose wherein the corrupt nation judged its corrupt judges. As Chazal said: "If [the judge] said to a man, 'Take the splinter from between your teeth,' he would retort, 'Take the beam from between your eyes' " (*Bava Basra* 15b). By speaking thus, one is in effect "judging the Judge," whereas the latter should be the one judging the people. It is this double affliction that Scripture is lamenting, as explained by our Sages: "Woe to the generation that judged its Judges, and woe to the generation whose Judges need to be judged." Woe to the generation for both reasons, for there is no difference whether the rock falls onto the pitcher or the pitcher onto the rock; in both cases the pitcher will break.

Thus, in one short phrase that complements the statement in the *Book of Judges* (2:17), "But they did not heed their judges either," the prophet portrays an uncivilized condition that has shaken to the foundation one of the pillars on which the world stands (*Avos* 1:18). Undermining the foundation of "Justice" hurts the Jewish nation especially, for its existence is premised on the implementation of law and justice. As we are commanded in the Torah: "You shall appoint for yourselves judges and policemen.... You shall strive after supreme justice, so that you will live and take possession of the land..." (*Devarim* 16:18–20).

Chazal say: "It is worthwhile to appoint upright judges to keep Israel alive and to settle them upon their land" (*Sifrei* and Rashi to *Devarim* ibid.). According to the rules by which the Torah is expounded, one may infer the negative from the positive: During the degenerate situation that prevailed "when the Judges governed," the Torah's warning came true, as the nation's life upon its land was destroyed.

"And There Was a Famine in the Land"

Scripture does not state how the famine arrived, its cause and effect — whether dishonesty and inflation led to financial ruin (see beginning of *Midrash Ruth Rabbah*), or by drastic changes in nature, as the Torah has warned, "Be careful that your hearts do not entice [you]...and He will close up the heavens" (*Devarim* 11:16–17), or by both methods. In any event, the situation reached the lowest point, as described in *Eichah* (4:9): "Those slain by the sword were more fortunate than those who died of hunger."

The expression, "there was a famine in the land," embraces all the conceptions of "famine," including its spiritual sense, which entails a physical hunger as well, as the Sages have said: "Why is 'vayehi' written twice? One is for the famine [due to the lack] of bread, and the other for the famine [due to the lack] of Torah. The lesson is that 'a generation that lacks Torah will not lack famine' " (*Midrash Zuta*). It appears that the statement does not mean that famine comes solely as a punishment to the generation that lacks Torah; rather, it comes as a result of the emptiness in which that generation is living. The Torah's promise, "You will eat and be satisfied," stated in the passage, "And it will be, if you constantly heed" (*Devarim* 11:15), is a blessing in and of itself: Man will come to be content and satisfied. At the time of moral decline, when man loses control and gives in to his desires, he will constantly be in a state of hunger. Perhaps this is the "tenth hunger" about which Chazal said that it "happens and comes to earth." In other words, it is the shadow that accompanies the emptying of one's soul, as it is written, "The deceptive soul will go hungry" (*Mishlei* 19:15; see Introduction).

The People's Hope

In those days of confusion and hopelessness, when communal life as well as individuals' lives were shattered, and both body and soul suffered from hunger, only one glimmer of hope remained: Perhaps one of the people's great persons would assume the leadership and even risk his own life to save the floundering ship. The people of Israel still remembered their first redeemer, Moshe Rabbenu, who had always been able to stop up the breaches that threatened to destroy the nation. Indeed, during their greatest emergency, when divine justice was about to strike out against the very survival of the Jewish nation, he threw himself into the breach and declared, "But if not, please erase me from Your Book that You have written" (*Shemos* 32:32). It is also written: "He said that He would destroy them, had not Moshe, His chosen one, stood in the breach before Him, to turn back His wrath from destroying" (*Tehillim* 106:23). Here Israel stands once again on the edge of the abyss, on the verge of destruction. Will they again merit a deliverer, a savior?

In fact, they did have someone on whom to pin their hopes. In the distinguished city of Israel, Beis Lechem Yehudah, then the seat of the Sanhedrin, lived a prominent, aristocratic family of Ephrathites (Ephrasim), "of the greats of the generation and its providers." The head of the family was preparing himself to become king of Israel, as his name implied: "Why was he called Elimelech? For he used to say,

'To me shall kingship come' " (*Chazal*). He had the right to it, because he was a descendant of Nachshon, son of Aminadav (*Bava Basra* 91a), the first prince of the tribe of Yehudah, to whom Ya'akov willed the kingship. Therefore, this was the man who, due to his high position and great influence, had been destined to extricate the nation from its distress.

"A [Great] Man from Beis Lechem Yehudah Went"

But Elimelech, the hope of all Israel, arises and leaves his people and his country. And to where does he go? To Mo'av, Israel's sworn enemy from the time of the exodus from Egypt; to Mo'av, against which the Torah had erected a permanent barrier: "No Ammoni or Mo'avi may enter [in marriage with a woman of] the congregation of the Eternal...because they did not offer you bread and water..." (*Devarim* 23:4–5). Elimelech and his family leave their people, who are convulsing in pain, for wicked and selfish neighbors. The captain abandoned the sinking ship, and escaped with his family in such a disraceful manner! It is easy to imagine how despondent those who remained on the ship must have felt as the storms arose to sink it in the depths! Our Sages gave the following description: "He caused Israel to lose heart" (*Ruth Rabbah* 1:4).

The utter possibility of the people's leader — he who was designated to be king — escaping, served as the last link in the condition of "the days when the Judges were judged" and as the most extreme manifestation of the situation that prevailed among the people. For what is the meaning of "A man did whatever was proper in his eyes" (*Shofetim* 17:6; 21:25), pointed out by the prophet *twice* in the Book of Judges? It does not imply that everyone harmed one another; rather, there was a lack of education for mutual responsibility, that one must confine one's own rights for those of the common good. Apparently, there existed then a certain rule that limiting personal freedom was forbidden, and that every man had the right to do "whatever was proper [הישר] in his eyes." That was the standard of that era. There is even an opinion among our Sages that it is the Book of Judges which is called the Book of Yashar (ספר הישר) for that reason (*Avodah Zarah* 25a). Were it not for that error — which had become so firmly established among the people of that generation — it would have been impossible for Elimelech to leave his country under such circumstances, for the leadership would have prevented it (see *Akeidas Yitzchak*).

The determination that the interests of the individual outweigh communal ones, was called by our Sages, "Elimelech's selfishness." And because he had this attribute, he was inclined to go to the land of Mo'av, where selfishness ruled!

Selfishness is the opposite of the attribute of kindness. The nation's lack of kindness toward its leader Yehoshua bin Nun at the beginning of the period, during blessed times (see Introduction), reached its climax at the end of the period, with the departure of the leader during bad times. This turned bad into worse, for Elimelech's action served as a tremor under the people's feet.

We may conclude that Scripture is describing three terrible calamities in the lives of the nation, each connected to the others, and each a result of the preceding one:

"And it was in the days when the Judges governed" — a moral and societal calamity;

"And there was a famine in the land" — a calamity of economic and related matters;

"A [great] man from Beis Lechem...went" — a calamity that removed the last glimmer of hope that still flickered in the people's hearts, and "caused Israel to lose heart."

(ב) וְשֵׁם הָאִישׁ אֱלִימֶלֶךְ וְשֵׁם אִשְׁתּוֹ נָעֳמִי וְשֵׁם שְׁנֵי־בָנָיו ׀ מַחְלוֹן וְכִלְיוֹן אֶפְרָתִים מִבֵּית לֶחֶם יְהוּדָה וַיָּבֹאוּ שְׂדֵי־מוֹאָב וַיִּהְיוּ־שָׁם:

(2) *The man's name was Elimelech, and his wife's name was Naomi, and the names of his two sons were Machlon and*

Kilyon; they were Ephrathites [aristocrats] from Beis Lechem [in] Yehudah, and they came to the fields of Mo'av and stayed there.

AN INDICTMENT OF ELIMELECH AND HIS SONS

"Like Foxes Among the Ruins"

The situation is rendered more intelligible by the words of our Sages, who apply the following words of the prophet to Elimelech and his sons (*Yechezkel* 13:4–5): "Your prophets, O Israel, have been like foxes among the ruins. You did not ascend into the breaches and build a fence for the House of Israel" — "Just as the fox waits among the ruins, and when it sees people approaching, it scurries off in another direction, so have your prophets been like foxes; you did not ascend into the breaches like Moshe did" (*Pesichah* 5 to *Ruth Rabbah*). Being the leaders and providers of the generation, Elimelech and his sons should have learned from Moshe to stop up the breaches. Instead, they escaped from the breaches, like a fox running away in the direction where it will be free from being threatened by humans. Had they fulfilled their duty and guided the generation toward virtuous behavior, the situation might not have deteriorated to the point where they had to leave the country. We may conclude, therefore, that they alone caused the first two calamities, which brought about the third one. They are censured not only for leaving the Holy Land, but also for "the judgment of the Judges," and for the famine that was in the land. It all points to poor leadership, which eventually led to escaping the country.

What a great difference there was between the first leader of the tribe of Yehudah and his direct descendant, who aspired to the throne! Nachshon ben Aminadav jumped into the sea, setting an example of self-sacrifice to the nation; whereas Elimelech left them moaning, and escaped like a fleeing fox (as Chazal explained, above). He thereby showed how unfit he was to be king. Wearing the crown requires the attributes of a lion. The lion goes before the camp, blazing a trail, while the fox squints to either side and seeks a path by which to escape from the place of danger. Concerning David, we find: "Your servant has slain the lion and the bear" (*Shemuel I* 17:36). In like fashion, he went out against Golias, whom no Israelite man could face. The lion knows no fear, but girds itself with strength, leaping forth to wherever necessary. The fox, however, calculates how to escape with his life. The "Cub of Yehudah" turned, in the words of Chazal, into a fox — this is the essential meaning of the journeying of Elimelech, with his wife and children, to Mo'av.

Indications of Guilt

We do not find open criticism of the trip in the Megillah; it is stated simply as a fact: "There was a famine...a [great] man went." Chazal, however, with their great perception, were able to detect concealed criticism from the style of the narrative. Compare the detailed description of the travel of the returnees from Bavel, affectionately and with honor, to the extent that Scripture lists even their horses, mules, camels and donkeys (*Ezra* 2:66–67). Here, however, a family renowned for its prominence and wealth sets out on a trip, and the prophet devotes not one word to how they traveled, stating merely, "a man went" — "A stump," say the Sages, that is stripped and alone, without a title or any description of what he took. With such dishonor does the Megillah express its estimation of those who leave the Land of Israel (*Ruth Rabbah* 1:5).

Our Sages made another important inference from the fact that, at the outset, Scripture does not mention the sojourners' names: "A man went...he with his wife and two sons." Only later, in verse 2, are their identities revealed. In Yalkut Ruth we find: "Said Rabbi Perachyah: God was judging the world at that moment; the heavenly court was in place, and God was concealing [Elimelech], as it is stated, 'And a man went.' The Attribute of [Strict] Justice arose and mentioned his name, as it is written, 'The man's name was Elimelech.' The edict was then immediately pronounced upon him and his sons." These two verses do not complement each other; they rather manifest the swinging of the scales between innocence and guilt. It was Heaven's intention to judge them favorably; that is why the first verse concealed their names and tried to save them. The attribute of strict justice, however, turned the scales. The prophet then wrote for eternal memory: "The man's name was Elimelech...Ephrasim [aristocrats] from Beis Lechem Yehudah" — These people who ran away from the land were members of the Ephrathite family! Just as the moon, which was diminished, appears in that state for all to see, so has this family been identified in the Book of Books, to bear its shame for posterity.

A CASE FOR FAVORABLE JUDGMENT

We find that there was also a positive side to the sojourn of Elimelech and his sons. Indeed, how could it be that these men, who, in the estimation of Chazal, as stated above, were among the generation's greatest personalities — and, some add, among its most righteous and pious ones — would be capable of acting so disgracefully without a rational reason and motive?! In fact, the departure of Elimelech and his sons was caused by the famine, due to which one may leave the Land of Israel, according to the principle of "When there is a famine in town, withdraw your feet" (see *Ruth Rabbah* 1:4; *Bava Kamma* 60b). Accordingly, we see that our ancestors went down to Egypt during a famine. Additionally, besides the famine — or because of it — the security situation in the Land of Israel had been undermined (*Chazal*). Furthermore, they had originally left only "to sojourn in the fields of Mo'av," not to settle there.

"They Should Have Prayed for Compassion on Their Generation"

However, all these arguments are not enough to vindicate

Elimelech and his sons. For what is permissible to an individual is forbidden to the nation's leader, whose every action affects the people's spirit. He must weigh every step he takes, not only for themselves, but mainly in consideration of their influence. Elimelech's going "caused Israel to lose heart." Even the danger was not reason enough, for it is self-sacrifice that is expected of a leader. Moreover, responsibility for the turbulent situation that endangered the leaders' lives falls on the leaders themselves. They should have refined their generation and saved it from trouble by pleading for compassion, as the Sages said (*Bava Basra* 91b): "Rabbi Chiya bar Avin said in the name of Rabbi Yehoshua ben Korchah, God forbid [that Elimelech and his family should be condemned for leaving]; for had they found even only bran they would not have left. Why then were they punished? Because they should have prayed for compassion on their generation, but they did not do so; for it is said: 'When you cry, let them whom you have gathered deliver you' " (*Yeshayahu* 57:13).

In other words, even if they had been forced to leave, they had brought it on themselves by not having begged for mercy. This only reiterates Elimelech's and his sons' greatness, for they could have saved the generation by pleading for mercy. As we have seen above, the complaint against them was because they did not "stand in the breach" as Moshe had done. This implies that they had been vulnerable to such criticism, for "In accordance with the camel is the burden." (The greater the man the more is expected of him.) All this casts Elimelech and his sons in a new light.

Why then, after all, did they not beg for mercy? Apparently, even asking for compassion depends upon one's view of the nation's condition and the possibility of its rectification. Even the Prophet Yirmyahu said: "If only I had [just] a wayfarers' hostel in the desert, then I would leave my people and go away from them" (*Yirmyahu* 9:1). What is more, we find concerning the Prophet Hoshe'a: "The Holy One, blessed is He, said to Hoshe'a, 'Your children have sinned,' to which he should have replied, 'They are Your children, the children of Your favored ones, the children of Avraham, Yitzchak and Ya'akov; extend Your mercy to them.' Not only did he not say thus, but he said to Him: 'Master of the Universe, they are Yours; exchange them for a different nation' " (*Pesachim* 87a). Thus, there was a situation where even the prophets were despaired of Israel and thought their predicament was hopeless.

The very notion of begging for mercy before the God of Law and Justice is not so obvious. No'ach, to whom the Torah ascribes the title, "a righteous and perfect man" (*Bereshis* 6:9), did not conceive of asking for compassion for the generation of the flood. Not that he was heartless; rather he thought: "If the Master of the Universe decreed destruction on His world, who am I to appeal against His judgment?" However, it was counted against him, as Scripture states (*Yeshayahu* 54:9): "This is for Me [like the oath of] the waters of No'ach" — " The flood was ascribed to him because he did not plead for compassion."

The first person to beg for mercy was our Forefather Avraham. After hearing the decree against Sedom, he cried out to God: "Can it be that the Judge of the whole earth would not carry out justice?" (*Bereshis* 18:25) — "If You want a world, there can be no strict judgment, and if it is strict judgment that You desire, there will be no world" (*Bereshis Rabbah* 49:20). Because of that he is raised above all generations that preceded him, to the point where our Sages expounded concerning him: "You loved justice and disdained wickedness" — You loved to justify My creatures and you refused to condemn them — "therefore, God, your God, has anointed you with oil of joy, above your peers" (*Tehillim* 45:8; (*Bereshis Rabbah* ibid.)). According to Chazal, our Forefather Avraham, too, should have continued praying, rather than stopping. As we know, he stopped when he heard that there were not even ten righteous men in Sedom. Scripture states:

"The Eternal left when He had finished speaking to Avraham" (*Bereshis* 18:33) — "Once the defender became silent, the Judge went his way" (Rashi). God, so to speak, awaited additional words from Avraham, for he should have added, "Master of the Universe, I will be their atonement," but he did not say it. Moshe, however, who said, "but if not, please erase me from Your Book" (*Shemos* 32:32), showed the ideal way to plead for compassion. (See more regarding all this in the *Zohar, Bereshis, Vayera, Milu'im* 12). Such self-sacrifice was required also of Elimelech when trouble overtook the people of Israel in his days.

A similar situation prevailed in the beginning of the Era of the Judges, after Yehoshua's death, when things took a terrible turn for the worse for the Jewish people, as told in the Book of Judges (3:7–10): "The children of Israel did what was evil in the eyes of the Eternal...and He surrendered them to Cushan-rish'athayim...the Eternal raised a savior for the children of Israel and he saved them: Othniel ben Kenaz...and the spirit of the Eternal was upon him." The Targum explains: "The spirit of the Eternal — the spirit of prophecy." Rashi states in the name of the Tanchuma: "He judged Israel" — He looked at what God told Moshe in Egypt, "I have well seen [ראה ראיתי] the suffering of my people." What is the meaning of the two "seeings" (i.e. the use of the verb ראה twice)? God was telling him: I see that they are going to sin with the [golden] calf; nevertheless, I have seen the suffering of my people. This was expounded by Othniel ben Kenaz, who said: "Whether they are culpable or innocent, He has to save them." Othniel ben Kenaz, too, struggled with that problem, during Israel's sharp decline following Yehoshua's death. He had to consider whether Israel was deserving of redemption. After searching for the Torah way, he discovered the prophetic truth that he must in any case rescue his people. And this is what Chazal meant by: "The spirit of the Eternal was upon him — the spirit of prophecy."

This was not the case with Elimelech, who despaired of his generation, believing that they had no remedy and were unworthy of asking for mercy. It was this despair that led him to get up and go to Mo'av. Chazal ascribe his move to selfishness, attributing it to the inner, hidden motives that brought him to carry it out. His action was not only a result of his perspective, but the reverse is true as well: His outlook came to justify his action, one that was influenced by another factor, the desire to save himself and his family from the terrible situation Israel was in. The narrow philosophy he espoused was nothing other than selfishness. It was this mistaken view that concealed Elimelech's flawed motive for going, an act that he deemed astute, correct, and necessary.

From this we may conclude that his going had merit as well as fault, both reflected alternately through concealment and reference in the verses of the Megillah. What the Sages meant by, "God was concealing [Elimelech...but] the Attribute of [Strict] Justice arose and mentioned his name," is that while the Attribute of Justice did what it was supposed to, concealment too plays a significant role — that of giving forth vital signals regarding the chain of events described in the Megillah.

The Ways of Providence

Elimelech's journey culminated in two effects: one resulting from the fact that he was mentioned and tainted by the Attribute of Justice — that is, the open punishment he and his family received by being destroyed; the other attributable to the concealment connected to his favorable judgment — namely, the remarkable outcome that the flight taken out of despair of the Jewish people became a means for their salvation and rise to greatness for many generations to come.

This teaches us something extraordinary: On the one hand, people are responsible for their deeds, and they will be held accountable for them. On the other hand, divine providence uses the acts of humans to further its hidden intentions, which are sometimes contrary to the will of those who perform them. Note, for example, the sale of Yosef, where the tribes' (sons of Ya'akov) negative act turned into a blessing, as we find in the words of Chazal: "The sin of the tribes is remembered forever, but provided hope forever" (*Bereshis Rabbah* 84:16). Elsewhere, they said: "Said Rabbi Yehudah bar Shalom: 'The one sitting, in which the tribes sat united in their plot to sell their brother, provided sustenance for the world for seven years' " (*Tanchuma Ki Sisa* 2). Concealed in the tribes' plan to sell their brother was God's plan to raise a redeemer who would save the world during the years of famine. Yosef himself explained this to his brothers: "So now [you see], it was not you who sent me here but God" (*Bereshis* 45:8).

This teaching is also apparent in our Megillah: Elimelech's family, which went to Mo'av out of selfishness, became a magnet sent on a mission by God to draw from there Ruth, who was a paragon of kindness, to the Jewish people. The going itself, which brought untold suffering upon Elimelech's family, produced the foundation for the stock of Yishai, from whom came David, King of Israel, from whom will come the Mashiach who will redeem the Jewish people and all mankind. That is how God produces a blessing in disguise, light from darkness. On the other hand, we discover that there was a spark of light hidden in the darkness, and that the bitterness had within it the element to turn it sweet; otherwise, this would constitute creating something out of nothing. Elimelech's going, despite the fact that it was leading to utter destruction, also contained a positive seed, one that sprouted and grew into everlasting glory.

The above sheds remarkable light on the Masoretic tradition that Scripture mentions the phrase "A man...went" only twice: "A man from the House of Levi went" (*Shemos* 2:1), and "A man from Beis Lechem...went" (*Ruth* 1:1). This significant parallelism is explained by the Ba'al ha-Turim on the verse in Shemos: "Amram's going led to the coming of the first redeemer [Moshe], and this [Elimelech's] coming will bring the last redeemer [Mashiach]."

At first sight, these two goings, that occurred during such trying times for the people of Israel, seem to be opposites. At the time of Paroh's decree, all Israelite men divorced their wives, as stated in the Midrash, to avoid having any more sons. Amram's going, which was for the purpose of remarrying his wife, was a determined act against the people's despair; it encouraged the children of Israel to continue surviving, despite Paroh's harsh decrees. Elimelech, however, yielded to adversity and left his people. His going sowed instability and despair. Nevertheless, the going of Elimelech, which caused Israel to lose heart, also caused them to be ready to take advantage of any future positive occurrence. Thus it, too, eventually led to a raising of the Jewish people's spirits. The two goings differ greatly from one another: The step taken in the first was firm and confident, while that of the second was desperate and weak. Both, however, had far-reaching results, affecting all generations to come. The first going resulted in the birth of Moshe, who redeemed Israel from Egyptian bondage and brought the Torah down from Heaven to guide the world toward redemption from sin and harm. From the second going, the Mashiach will come forth, who will actually implement the redemption. Thus, the second going completes, through its outcome that came from an opposite direction, the first going, whose results came directly.

Sometimes great things are accomplished by one's own deeds, but sometimes a person becomes a catalyst to important events despite his actions. Both, however, may lead to the same results. Elimelech's family was privileged to work wonders only by way of the second method. The Megillah first tells about the evident connection between the going and its consequences.

2. And they came to the fields of Mo'av and stayed there.

From the plural, the fields of Mo'av, our Sages deduced that they spent time searching and wandering in Mo'av: "First they entered the towns, but found their inhabitants to be immoral. Then they came into the cities, but saw that they

suffered from water shortages. So they returned to the towns"
(*Ruth Rabbah* 2:6). Such a description also shows that this
family had laudable traits. It was due to moral and economic
reasons that it was difficult for them to find a suitable place.
When they resigned themselves to the local situation,
however, they became settlers there, although at the outset
they had gone only "to sojourn in the fields of Mo'av" (not to
settle there). Moreover, they adjusted to the new society and
assumed prominent positions therein, as the Targum
explains: "And they stayed [ויהיו — lit. became] there — they
became ministers there."

Here we see the difference between Ya'akov and his
children, and Elimelech and his children. Scripture describes
how Yosef presented before Paroh "[five men] from among
his [weaker] brothers" (*Bereshis* 47:2). Rashi explains: "From
those who were of lesser strength, who do not look strong,
for if they appear to him as strong, he would make them his
soldiers." Yosef took care that Paroh should not see that his
brothers might be useful in the service of Paroh's state, lest
they establish roots in Egypt. Here, on the other hand, we
find that the great men of Yehudah invested all their energy
in a foreign nation, at a time when they were sorely needed
by their own people. This is just another indication that they
possessed an attribute of Mo'av (selfishness), to the point that
they could even settle there and become ministers.

וַיָּמָת אֱלִימֶלֶךְ אִישׁ נָעֳמִי וַתִּשָּׁאֵר הִיא וּשְׁנֵי בָנֶיהָ: (ג)

(3) *Elimelech, Naomi's husband, then died, and she remained
[a widow], and her two sons [orphans].*

3. Elimelech, Naomi's husband, then died...

Here begins the punishment, striking the head of the
family first. Scripture captures the enormity of the tragedy of
his death in the two words, "Naomi's husband." Who is it that
died? Not the leader and provider of the generation, the
aspirant to royalty, but Naomi's husband. The leader who had
hoped to unite a nation became an insignificant person, one

whose death affected only his wife, because he had already been dead to his people. He who had been "Elimelech" ended his life as "Naomi's husband."

Look at what this man forfeited. Had he done his duty, his name would have been etched forever in the Book of Books as one who had endeavored to save the people of Israel from a famine. Now his name is inscribed as someone who fled. Besides, he failed to achieve even that which he attempted by his escape. He did not save his life, but died in an out-of-the-way, forsaken, foreign land. According to Chazal, he also became very impoverished before his death. This presents an important lesson about human greatness and human weakness: A person stands on the highest rungs of the spiritual and societal ladder, and instead of climbing higher, in a moment of weakness he steps backward, falls way down, and even drags his family behind him.

From here we see that even the greatest people are liable to stumble. Similarly, we learned in Avos (2:8): "Do not believe in yourself until the day you die." This principle applies to everyone, great or small.

And she remained [a widow], and her two sons [orphans]...

The Midrash (*Ruth Rabbah* 2:8) explains the word "remained" in terms of remnants, leftovers. Here we have a description of the private life of a Jewish family and of the significance of the head of the family. First Scripture points out the importance of each of them: "The man's name was Elimelech, and his wife's name was Naomi, and the names of his two sons were Machlon and Kilyon; they were Ephrasim [aristocrats] from Beis Lechem [in] Yehudah." Now, following the death of Elimelech, also his wife and sons have lost their importance; they are collectively merely remnants — she, a widow from her husband, and they, orphaned of their father. The Targum states explicitly: "And she remained a widow, and her two sons orphans." (Chazal derived from other verses [*Yalkut Shimoni Ruth, Remez* 600] that a person dies and leaves orphans only because of selfishness. Hence, there is an allusion in our verse to why Elimelech was punished.)

(ד) וַיִּשְׂאוּ לָהֶם נָשִׁים מֹאֲבִיּוֹת שֵׁם הָאַחַת עָרְפָּה וְשֵׁם הַשֵּׁנִית רוּת
וַיֵּשְׁבוּ שָׁם כְּעֶשֶׂר שָׁנִים:

(4) *They then married Mo'avi women — one's name was Orpah
and the other's name was Ruth — and they lived there for
about ten years.*

4. They then married Mo'avi women...

"It was taught in the name of Rabbi Meir: 'They neither
converted nor immersed them, nor had the Halachic
interpretation yet been expressed permitting a female
Ammoni or Mo'avi' " (*Yalkut Shimoni Ruth, Remez* 600). Rabbi
Meir's words are based on the wording of the passage: Mo'avi
women. This implies that they remained Mo'avi women even
after their marriage, for had they converted they would no
longer have been Mo'avi, since "one who has become a
proselyte is like a child newly born." And even if they had
converted, they would not have been able to build a Jewish
home, for the Halachic derivation permitting a female
Ammoni or Mo'avi had not yet been declared. These
marriages, then, were quite radical. As long as Elimelech was
alive, his sons did not intermarry. However, after his death,
his sons married Mo'avi women without even converting
them.

They could not have descended to such debasement as
attaching themselves to Mo'av had they not adopted the
Mo'avi trait [of selfishness] as Chazal noted: "What led them
to marry Mo'avi women? They practiced selfishness, as did
Ammon and Mo'av" (ibid.) Furthermore, the words "They
married [להם ויקחו — lit. they took unto themselves]"
underscores the fact that their very marriage was stamped
with selfishness. For marriage generally contains an element
of kindness, that of contributing to the building of the world,
whereas they disregarded the world around them and took
wives to satisfy only themselves; they were aware that their
children would not be allowed to marry within the fold, or be
counted as Jews. Thus, they isolated themselves in Mo'av:

"They lived there for about ten years" — apparently with no yearnings for their country, and with no intention to return. Happy with their family life, they forgot their people, their homeland, and their lineage. The exile that had originally been forced upon them they now came to accept willingly and without reserve. Thus, they went from bad to worse: from "[they] went to sojourn in the fields of Mo'av" to "and [they] stayed there," and from "and [they] stayed there" to "and they lived there." "They left Israel and joined the fields of Mo'av" — and no ordinary wind could uproot them from there. For this they were severely criticized, to the point that Scripture immortalized their names as "Machlon and Kilyon," because "they were completely wiped out [machoh] and terminated [kaloh] from the world." They were also called "Yo'ash and Saraf" (*Divrei HaYamim* I 4:22), because "they lost hope [ya'osh] in the redemption and 'burned' [sarof] the Torah" (by neglecting it; see *Ruth Rabbah* 2:4). Because they had utterly despaired and burned behind them all bridges that had connected them to the Jewish people, they had become Machlon and Kilyon.

(ה) וַיָּמֻתוּ גַם־שְׁנֵיהֶם מַחְלוֹן וְכִלְיוֹן וַתִּשָּׁאֵר הָאִשָּׁה מִשְּׁנֵי יְלָדֶיהָ וּמֵאִישָׁהּ:

(5) *Both Machlon and Kilyon also died, and the woman remained [bereft] of her two children and her husband.*

5. Both Machlon and Kilyon also died...

"Do not say that selfishness strikes down only the fathers" (*Chazal*). From the word "also" our Sages deduced that they died [for the same reason] as Elimelech died. And since Elimelech had died because of the selfishness that had caused him to leave the land of Israel, so did his sons die on account of that sin, and not because they had wed gentile women. In addition to informing us that "both [sons] died," Scripture adds their names, "Machlon and Kilyon," to emphasize that their deaths had the purpose of "wiping out" and "terminating" them, that is, totally uprooting them from the House of Israel. This, then, was the fate of Elimelech and his sons: They had gone to Mo'av to save themselves, but not only did they not succeed in saving themselves, they severed their lineage and aspirations to royalty as well. What is more, they unknowingly handed over their lost crown to a gentile woman. Here we see the sin and its punishment. Yet, how wonderful are the ways of divine providence, for these men, who had abandoned the people of Israel in disgrace, and did not merit having even one word of theirs recorded in the Bible, are the ones who indirectly inspirited not only Israel, but all humankind. That was the concealed outcome of their going, upon which the entire following story of the Megillah revolves.

And the woman remained [bereft] of her two children and her husband...

"Said Rabbi Chanina, 'She was like the remnants of the remnants' " (*Ruth Rabbah* 2:10). In concise language, Scripture here presents this woman as a second Iyov, who had lost all her property and honor, and buried her entire family in a foreign land. By twice mentioning "and she remained," Scripture stresses another point: that from the entire family this woman alone remained, to fulfill a messianic role through which her name would become immortalized. She was able to attain that because of her lofty attributes, which are implied in her very name: "Naomi [נעמי] — for her deeds were pleasing and sweet [נעימים]" (*Ruth Rabbah* 3:7). As the Megillah unfolds, she plays a respectable role through her actions and words. The fact that the prophet recorded her for posterity shows that they obviously have enduring value.

וַתָּקָם הִיא וְכַלֹּתֶיהָ וַתָּשָׁב מִשְׂדֵי מוֹאָב כִּי שָׁמְעָה בִּשְׂדֵה מוֹאָב (ו)
כִּי־פָקַד יְהֹוָה אֶת־עַמּוֹ לָתֵת לָהֶם לָחֶם:

(6) *She then arose, with her daughters-in-law, [to] return from the fields of Mo'av, for she heard in the field of Mo'av that the*

Eternal had taken account of His people to provide them with food.

6. She then arose...

This statement does not pertain to her actual going from Mo'av, since that is discussed in the next verse. Rather, it is referring to the important decision that preceded that act, and that resulted from introspection that enabled her to understand how her whole life had been shattered. It must have been difficult for her to arrive at such a decision. For she knew where she was heading: to disgrace and poverty that awaited her in Yehudah, as described later in the Megillah. After having come to the realization, however, that she must make amends, she surmounted all inner and outer impediments, shook herself loose as a lion, and arose, the latter word implying industriousness (see *Alshich* and *Iggeres Shemuel*). Sometimes the Scriptural verb "to arise" suggests rising from the lowly, rectification and elevation, as in the comment of the Sages to the verse (*Bereshis* 23:17) "The field of Efron was transferred [ויקם — lit. 'and it rose']": "It had fallen and arisen" (*Bereshis Rabbah* 58:10; see Rashi there). The field had a rise (in importance) as it was transferred from the hands of Efron to those of Avraham, and acquired everlasting prominence as the Machpelah Cave. How instructive is our Sages' comment on our verse, "She [Naomi] then arose": "She had fallen, but she raised herself up by returning to the Land of Israel" (*Midrash Lekach Tov*). During the period of the moral decline of Elimelech's family, Naomi had regressed along with them, for in the beginning there is no indication in Scripture of any intention of hers to return; she had been as liable to be destroyed as the rest of her family. Ultimately, however, she made her courageous decision, thus providing a permanent recovery to herself and, in a roundabout way, to the whole family as well. Through their very going to Mo'av, she acquired her hidden importance, which continues and reveals itself before us in the Megillah. From this arising of the "fallen" Naomi begins the ascending line that leads to David's birth.

For she heard in the field of Mo'av that the Eternal had taken account of His people to provide them with food...

From the wording it is clear that she heard not only the simple fact that there was already food in Yehudah; she heard also the reason for it: "that the Eternal had taken account of His people," with the accent on "His people." They had been punished by famine for acting as "not His people." The affliction succeeded in effecting a transformation in the Jewish people, regarding whom the following became fulfilled: "And I will say to Lo-Ami [Not My People], 'You are Ami [My People]' " (*Hoshe'a* 2:25). Consequently, the famine passed, a situation to which Chazal attributed the passage, "for the Eternal does not forsake His people." This affords us some insight into the reason why Elimelech and his family ran away and why Naomi returned: They despaired of the Jewish people, whereas she saw that the nation had gone back to what it should be, meaning that the escape had been a blunder!

All the same, we see that prior to her finding out that "the Eternal had taken account of His people," Naomi did not do any soul-searching, nor did she become inspired to return to the Land of Israel, despite all the misfortune that befell Elimelech's household, herself included. The same may even be said of our Forefather Ya'akov: Esav had wanted to kill him; he took all the gifts Ya'akov had sent him; Esav's guardian angel tried to kill him and managed to injure his hip; then came the misfortunes regarding Dinah and Rachel. And throughout all this Ya'akov did not feel that he was being punished for not having fulfilled the vow he had made at Beis El, until finally: "God said, 'How long will this righteous man be punished without realizing what it is for? I will make it known to him,' as it is written: God then said to Ya'akov, 'Arise, go up to Beis El' " (*Tanchuma Vayishlach* 9). If that is the case, we may understand how difficult it is for one to perform a personal stock-taking and to determine whether, or for what, he is liable.

וַתֵּצֵא מִן־הַמָּקוֹם אֲשֶׁר הָיְתָה־שָּׁמָּה וּשְׁתֵּי כַלּוֹתֶיהָ עִמָּהּ וַתֵּלַכְנָה (ז)
בַדֶּרֶךְ לָשׁוּב אֶל־אֶרֶץ יְהוּדָה:

(7) *She left the place where she was [living], with her two daughters-in-law, and they went on the road to return to the land of Yehudah.*

7. She left the place where she was [living]...

"Rabbi Azaryah said in the name of Rabbi Yehudah bar Simon: The greatest man in the city is its splendor, its glory, its majesty, and its grandeur. But when he departs from there, its splendor, glory, majesty, and grandeur depart. And this is what happened when Ya'akov left Be'er Sheva" (*Ruth Rabbah* 2:12). Chazal's comment is based on the fact that the passage about Naomi's departure seems superfluous, in light of the preceding statement, "She...return[ed] from the fields of Mo'av." It must be, therefore, that Scripture is using the special expression employed to describe the departure of great people, as in "Ya'akov left Be'er Sheva" (*Bereshis* 28:10; see Rashi there). This comes to teach us the importance of the righteous, who influence their place in many good ways, and whose departure is apparent in all areas of life and felt by all. It is similar to a great mural decorating a palace: Removing it denudes the wall. This is what is meant by the expression, "She left the place" — she left a void; the place she had left became reduced to orphanhood.

With her two daughters-in-law — Three women stricken with the same fate, each of them forlorn and broken, together setting out on a long journey in great poverty, without even shoes to wear, as Chazal explained (*Ruth Rabbah* 2:12) the expression "and they went on the road." They headed for the Land of Yehudah, where nothing but poverty, misery and disgrace awaited them. Nevertheless, their going did not have the same meaning to the three of them. Naomi was returning to her country, being drawn there by an abundance of memories, yearnings, feelings of regret and repentance. She was advanced in years, and had no more demands on life except settling her accounts with the past. Her two young daughters-in-law, however, were leaving their homeland, the place of their roots and ancestors, where their lives had been firmly established, and where they would be able to go back and build their future. Yet, they were giving up all that and going to an unfamiliar country. They surely knew that they would have to subsist from gleanings of the fields! And why did they go to such lengths? Solely not to be separated from their elderly, depressed mother-in-law and not to leave her alone in her bitter sorrow.

Light of kindness was planted on the steps of these two daughters of Mo'av, indirectly casting rays of light backward also, onto Machlon and Kilyon, who were already beyond the horizon. Their inner family life has been concealed by the Megillah, but from their widows' dedication to their mother-in-law, we may imagine how much innocence and pleasantness suffused the family life of those two aristocrats of Yehudah. Otherwise, it is impossible to understand the strong ties that bound the women to that family. Consequently, Machlon and Kilyon play a role in the chain of events that followed their death, so that by speaking evil of them we have also come to praise them. The main power of attraction, however, came from Naomi (נעמי), "who was pleasant [נעימה] in word and deed" (*Ruth Rabbah* 3:7). Hence, Orpah and Ruth were drawn to her as two planets gravitating towards the sun.

(ח) וַתֹּאמֶר נָעֳמִי לִשְׁתֵּי כַלֹּתֶיהָ לֵכְנָה שֹּׁבְנָה אִשָּׁה לְבֵית אִמָּהּ יַעֲשֶׂה (יַעַשׂ ק') יְהֹוָה עִמָּכֶם חֶסֶד כַּאֲשֶׁר עֲשִׂיתֶם עִם־הַמֵּתִים וְעִמָּדִי: (ט) יִתֵּן יְהֹוָה לָכֶם וּמְצֶאןָ מְנוּחָה אִשָּׁה בֵּית אִישָׁהּ וַתִּשַּׁק לָהֶן וַתִּשֶּׂאנָה קוֹלָן וַתִּבְכֶּינָה: (י) וַתֹּאמַרְנָה־לָּהּ כִּי־אִתָּךְ נָשׁוּב לְעַמֵּךְ:

(8) *Naomi then said to her two daughters-in-law, "Go, return, each to your mother's house. May the Eternal treat you kindly, just as you treated the deceased and [treated] me.* (9) *May the*

Eternal grant you that each find contentment in her husband's home." She then kissed them, and they began crying loudly. (10) They said to her, "[No,] for we will return with you to your people."

8. Naomi then said to her two daughters-in-law, "Go, return..."

From Naomi's words we can feel Naomi's abundant sympathy and pureness. She refrains completely from speaking of her own misfortune, seeking happiness only for her daughters-in-law, refusing to have them sacrifice anything for her. However, from the fact that she asked them three times to "return," our Sages learned the Halachah that a potential convert is dissuaded up to three times.

In Naomi's first statement there is an additional word, "Go, return," in which our Sages detected — beside a wish for the happiness of the daughters-in-law and the repelling of proselytes — another inner voice of Naomi: "Go!" This word, which seems to be extra, reflects her hidden desire that they go back. As our Sages note: "Why is she sending them back? — So she will not be embarrassed by them (*Yalkut Shimoni Remez* 601).When she first conjured up the picture of herself, Naomi, wife of Elimelech and mother of aristocratic sons, returning to Beis Lechem with two gentile daughters-in-law, a feeling of shame sneaked into her heart. This feeling found expression in the word "Go."

9. May the Eternal grant you...

Apparently, she had already expressed her blessing with the words, "May the Eternal treat you kindly," since God knows how much reward one deserves: "And your Employer can be relied on to pay you the reward for your work" (*Avos* 2:16). If the Megillah's author quotes Naomi as adding, "May the Eternal grant you," it must be that these words contain something new, something that was not implied in the previous blessing. The Targum hints at its meaning by adding: "full reward." Our Sages explained it as referring to [Naomi's future descendant, King] Shelomo: "May the Eternal grant you" — Said Rabbi Yosei, "From you shall come all the favors and gifts that God will grant Shelomo, as it is written: God granted wisdom to Shelomo" (*Ruth Rabbah* 2:15). This appears to be difficult, for was Naomi a prophetess who knew what God was going to give Shelomo?

The explanation is as follows: Naomi sees an unmatched degree of kindness in the behavior of her daughters-in-law. The typical reward of a life of bliss that God bestows on deserving people would not be sufficient for them. Therefore, she says, "May the Eternal grant you," emphasizing the word you: May He give you something new that has never been given before, something that is beyond ordinary earthly grants. Scripture specifies this new thing as the wisdom that was granted to Shelomo, concerning whom it is stated: "He was the wisest of all people." Our Sages are highlighting here not only his wisdom, but all the good and relief that Shelomo brought to the world. Shelomo symbolizes eternal peace and brotherhood, by the Temple that he built for Israel as well as the nations. And these are the foundations that will bring mankind to perfection in the time of the Mashiach. Because Naomi sees in their deeds roots of perfection, she blesses them with: "May...grant you — all the favors and gifts that God will grant Shelomo." Hence, these words of Naomi contain not merely a blessing, but mainly an appraisal, as if to say: You are worthy of having the ultimate gift — that which is stored by the King of the Universe for man who is created in His image — come out of you. It is amazing that Naomi gives the same commendation to both her daughters-in-law. Even she had not yet noticed the difference between them. What is much more astonishing is that she, of the family of the leaders of the tribe of Yehudah, from whom it was prophesied that the Mashiach would arise, would give this blessing to gentile women, of the nation of Mo'av, no less! It is as though she were verifying that they were worthy of it. How much modesty and magnanimity Naomi's statement contains, words inspired by divine inspiration. Not undeservedly was she called Naomi [נעמי] for she acted pleasantly [נעימה] in both word and deed.

(יא) וַתֹּאמֶר נָעֳמִי שֹׁבְנָה בְנֹתַי לָמָּה תֵלַכְנָה עִמִּי הַעוֹד־לִי בָנִים בְּמֵעַי וְהָיוּ לָכֶם לַאֲנָשִׁים: (יב) שֹׁבְנָה בְנֹתַי לֵכְןָ כִּי זָקַנְתִּי מִהְיוֹת לְאִישׁ כִּי אָמַרְתִּי יֶשׁ־לִי תִקְוָה גַּם הָיִיתִי הַלַּיְלָה לְאִישׁ וְגַם יָלַדְתִּי בָנִים: (יג) הֲלָהֵן | תְּשַׂבֵּרְנָה עַד אֲשֶׁר יִגְדָּלוּ הֲלָהֵן תֵּעָגֵנָה לְבִלְתִּי הֱיוֹת לְאִישׁ אַל בְּנֹתַי כִּי־מַר־לִי מְאֹד מִכֶּם כִּי־יָצְאָה בִי יַד־יְהֹוָה:

(11) *Naomi answered [them], "Return, my daughters. Why do you [wish to] go with me? Do I have any more sons in my womb [who] could become your husbands?! (12) Return, my daughters, go, for I am too old to marry a man [and bear children]. [Even] if I would say [to myself] there is hope for me; even [if] I were to marry a man tonight [and conceive]; or even [if] I had [already] borne sons — (13) for them would you wait in anticipation until they grow up?! For them would you remain bound by not marrying another man?! No, my daughters, for my [situation] is much more bitter than yours, for the Eternal's plague has affected me."*

11. Naomi answered [them], "Return, my daughters..."

This is the first time we hear her say "my daughters." Their answer, "for we will return with you to your people," caused her to relate to them in this new way. Yet, she still turns them away, as the Halachah requires concerning potential converts, for we do not know what is in another person's mind; perhaps strange thoughts are brewing there. This course of action proved itself in that, whereas Orpah and Ruth had been of the same mind, Orpah changed hers and followed Naomi's suggestion.

Do I have any more sons in my womb — It seems like Naomi is overstating her case. In truth, however, her words contain good psychology. To justify one's hopes, a person may give flight to his imagination, as a wise man once said: "Man is free with his imagination." In order that her daughters-in-law's decisions be free of illusory or false considerations, Naomi attempted, by using exaggeration, to rid them of any illusions and to explain to them that there is no way they will find rest in Yehudah, as Chazal so aptly put it: A woman has no satisfaction except in her husband's home (*Ruth Rabbah* 2:16). Therefore, they can expect mental suffering, which would be burdensome, rather than helpful, to Naomi. For not only would she not be comforted by them, but they would add to her sorrow whenever she saw their own pain.

13. For my [situation] is much more bitter than yours...

Naomi summarizes the futility of their accompanying her, with the following words, "for the Eternal's plague has affected me" — The Attribute of Justice has already spent itself against me, so that no human kindness can heal me. The Seder Olam draws an analogy from the verse, "Whenever they would go out, the hand of the Eternal would be against them for evil" (*Shofetim* 2:15). In other words, God's hand will find me in any event; hence, you will not help me by going with me, since I am among those who are beyond hope. Here we discern the bitterness of the despair of Naomi, who has acquired the tribulations of Iyov. Though she did not sit in mourning [lit. in ashes] as he did, she carried [the ashes of] her mourning in her heart.

(יד) וַתִּשֶּׂנָה קוֹלָן וַתִּבְכֶּינָה עוֹד וַתִּשַּׁק עָרְפָּה לַחֲמוֹתָהּ וְרוּת דָּבְקָה בָּהּ:

(14) *They began [lit. lifted (ותשנה) their voice] crying loudly again. Orpah then kissed her mother-in-law [farewell], while Ruth clung to her.*

14. They began crying loudly again.

The word ותשנה is written without the customary א (ותשאנה). Our Sages explain: "They became weak from walking and crying" (*Ruth Rabbah* 2:21). Both Orpah and Ruth were struck dumb following Naomi's strong and bitter words, and they began to cry. Despite their tears, however, which were apparently equally sincere, the two sisters parted ways.

Orpah then kissed her mother-in-law [farewell], while Ruth clung to her. — How could they have come to such opposite decisions after they both had heard the same words of

Naomi? It must be because each had listened differently. It would appear that Orpah is the one who listened to Naomi and followed her request, whereas Ruth made up her own mind. Our Sages, however, state the opposite: "Why was she called 'Orpah' [עָרְפָּה] Because she turned her back [עָרֶף] on her mother-in-law. And 'Ruth' [רוּת]? Because she understood [lit. saw (רָאֲתָה)] what her mother-in-law was saying." For Naomi, in the course of repelling them, twice calls them "my daughters" instead of "my daughters-in-law." In this motherly word, that emanates from the depths of her heart, an invitation lies hidden, for a mother does not push away her daughters. The sweet tone that resonated in Naomi's words reached Ruth's ears, but not Orpah's. Orpah did not hear Naomi's words with her inner ear, the ear of her soul, or else her soul lacked the fine filament that Naomi's words could vibrate. Moreover, she took Naomi's words as a rebuke: "For my [situation] is much more bitter than yours [מִכֶּם — lit. 'because of you']" — "All the misfortune has befallen me because of you."

The big difference between them was thus first observed in the way each had listened, for until then they had appeared to be equals in merit and spiritual attributes. Naomi's words served as the test that revealed how the daughters-in-law differed from each other and in the level of their devotion to her. Orpah's eventual turning of her back on her mother-in-law showed that she had not been as close to her as Ruth had. Orpah had been bound to her mother-in-law only superficially, but not with her innermost feelings, which only now revealed themselves. Consequently, Naomi's kiss, too, had different meanings to each of them. Naomi's kisses were not yet meant to impart farewell. Deep down, she did not want to separate; she had acted shrewdly, as one who "pushes away with the left hand and draws near with the right." Orpah, however, with her hidden desire to depart, interpreted it as a good-bye kiss. Ruth, on the other hand, reacted to the kiss as if it were dew descending on a blossoming flower, intensifying its freshness and fragrance.

On Orpah, though, it had the effect of dew falling on a flower that had begun to wilt; it merely hastens its withering.

When the time arrived for Orpah to kiss her mother-in-law, she spent all that remained of her love and devotion with that kiss. Chazal (*Ruth Rabbah* 2:22) enumerate several types of kisses: "A kiss of eminence, such as that given by Shemuel to Sha'ul when he anointed him king; a kiss of [meeting after] periods [of separation], such as that of Aharon and Moshe (*Shemos* 4:27): "He went and met him at the Mountain of God and kissed him"; and a kiss of separation: "Orpah then kissed her mother-in-law." That is to say, there is a kiss that strengthens the bond between two people — for example, the kiss of Moshe and Aharon. Then there is a kiss that severs the connection that existed between two souls. A clear example of the latter is the kiss of Orpah, who uses it to turn her back on her mother-in-law and on her entire former way of life, a way in which she had been following her mother-in-law in order to get closer to the Jewish people. Orpah returns to her Mo'avi roots that seethe with an ancient hatred toward the Jews. The sons of Orpah, according to a tradition of Chazal (*Sotah* 42b), soon took up arms against the Jews. Golias the Philistine — also a son of hers — disgraced the battalions of the Living God forty days.

Even Orpah, however, initially followed Naomi, shedding tears when she separated from her. Chazal, realizing that tears do not go to waste, ascribed the following verse to them (*Shemuel II* 21:22): "These four were born to the Raphah [giant] in Gas" — "Said Rava, 'In the merit of the four tears Orpah shed over her mother-in-law, she was privileged to have four warriors descend from her' " (*Sotah* 42b).

Chazal shared another insight: "Rabbi Yitzchak said, 'Orpah accompanied her mother-in-law a distance of four *mil*, and was rewarded by having four warriors descend from her.'" Also Orpah displayed strength, for such an act of dedication takes courage. Therefore, she deserved Naomi's blessing along with Ruth: "May the Eternal grant you that each...." She cried because she had to separate from her, a sign of an inner struggle that led to her meriting warriors. "Warrior" in the Bible implies also spiritual powers, for the strong sprout solely from a source of strength.

In fact, Orpah and Ruth stemmed from the same root. Both were daughters of Eglon, King of Mo'av, who is represented in Scripture as exemplifying respect for God's word (*Shofetim 3:20; see Yalkut Shimoni Shofetim, Remez* 247). It was from their distant ancestresses, the daughters of Lot, that they inherited the worthy trait of self-sacrifice to build the world. Both their souls were molded from the same matter, but not of equal quality. One's character was perfect — no power on earth could obstruct it — while the other's was finite. Orpah gave in when the pressure became too hard for her to bear. At first she apparently had a glitter of hope that she would be able to rebuild her life in Yehudah as well. Naomi's penetrating words, however, left no room for self-delusion. It immediately aroused her hidden ego, which emerged and overpowered her attribute of kindness, the latter which requires total submission of one's ego for the benefit of others. The kiss she gave her mother-in-law was the act with which she finally dissipated her striving. The same remarkable spiritual strength that had given rise to her former determination to follow Naomi now aroused a counterforce that drove her in the opposite direction. Our Sages relate that from the very same day when she parted ways with her mother-in-law, Orpah adopted a perverted lifestyle in the extreme (see *Sotah* 42b). Concerning Ruth, however, not only did her resolve not fade away during the last test, it actually became even stronger!

Yet, we must deal with the following difficulty: Was there still a need for them to accompany Naomi after they had heard her say that there was no purpose or benefit involved, and that their sacrifice would be for naught? For this is similar to the problem posed by the well-known *baraisa* (*Bava Metzia* 62a): Two men were traveling in the desert, and one had a pitcher of water. If both drink, they will both die, but if only one drinks, he can reach civilization. Ben Petura taught: It is better that both should drink and die, than that one should see his companion's death. Until Rabbi Akiva came and taught (*Vayikra* 25:36): "that your brother may live *with* you" — your life takes precedence over his life.

"Your life takes precedence" — That is society's standard, and how Orpah acted. When she discovered that there was no reason or rationale for self-sacrifice, she decided to return. She could not surmount the obstacles; only Ruth displayed such strength. Ruth's chosen path was not for everyone, only for a select few. The truth of human logic prevailed over Orpah's dedication. A different truth, however, predominated in Ruth's soul, a prophetic truth that bypasses narrow logic, far overtaking it by gigantic steps, on the path that leads to the betterment of the world. The power that kept Ruth next to Naomi was her devotedness — "Ruth clung to her."

In both Orpah and Ruth's heart there was a violin that played a melody of kindness. Naomi's pressure, however, broke one of Orpah's violin strings. One day, that same broken violin would play the words of Golias the Philistine. The chord in Ruth's heart, however, gave out even more refined notes under Naomi's pressure, eventually becoming a chord of the world-renowned violin on which the "Sweet Singer of Israel" (David) would play. "Why was she called Ruth [רות]? Because David, who satisfied [רוה] the Holy One, blessed is He, was her descendant" (*Bava Basra* 14b). The phrase "who satisfied the Holy One, etc.," means that God does not require from man more than that which was expressed in David's songs. And the root from which David's singing sprouted was hidden in Ruth's soul.

At first, both Orpah and Ruth accompanied Naomi as two planets gravitating toward the sun. It later became clear, however, that Orpah was merely like a meteor that flared, flickered, and fell to the ground in the form of Golias the Philistine and his three brothers, as it is written: "These four were born to the Raphah in Gas" (*Shemuel II*, 21:22). It causes destruction where it falls, but it would always remain a scorched stone. In contrast, Ruth's star will shine forever in the form of the man whose "name will endure as long as the sun" (*Tehillim* 72:17).

RUTH AND ORPAH, DAVID AND GOLIAS, ISRAEL AND THE NATIONS

There is a silent conflict between "Orpah then kissed her mother-in-law" and "Ruth clung to her." Orpah's parting kiss says: An idea has to embellish and improve life. However, the life of one who possesses that idea need not be sacrificed for it. If going with Naomi demands such a sacrifice, it is not for Orpah. Her own welfare comes first, a decision that is justified from a humanitarian viewpoint. In Ruth's eyes, though, one's convictions outweigh one's life, and they are acquired through self-sacrifice. Here lies a higher truth — one that is hidden from view, clashes with private gain, and is obvious. But it will ultimately prevail. The same conflict between the kiss and the clinging would be reflected generations later in the battle between Golias and David.

ଔ   ଔ   ଔ

It is superficial to say that the duel between David and Golias consisted of a spiritual force opposing a totally physical one. In Golias, too, there existed a noticeable spirituality. First, we see that he wished to prevent futile bloodshed by suggesting only a duel. Also from his words, as recorded in Scripture as well as those transmitted to us by our Sages, we hear not the voice of someone who is an expert only in the flashing of swords; he talks rather as a person who knows how to speak wisely and cleverly. It is not for nothing that his words and reasoning are recorded — something Scripture refrains from doing anywhere else, except in connection with the battle of Yiftach. Golias calls out to the ranks of Israel (*Shemuel I* 17:8; see also Targum and Rashi): "Why should you go forth to wage war? Am I not the Philistine, and you Sha'ul's servants?" He enumerates the wars he fought and his victories, all done despite his not having become a general or a commander. In other words, he participates in his nation's wars as a volunteer Philistine patriot, without coercion or expecting any reward. On the other hand, in the Jewish army, external means are necessary to motivate its men to acts of bravery. In this war as well, it has been announced that whoever smites Golias will receive great wealth from Sha'ul, "and he will exempt his father's family in Israel" (ibid. v. 25). He is comparing the freedom under his government to the oppressive regime of Israel.

Golias' arguments are not limited to the above. Chazal explain his cry, "Give me a man and we will fight together" (ibid. v. 8), as follows: "A Man" refers to God, concerning Whom it is stated, "The Eternal is a Man of War." Thus he is also attacking the veracity of the God of Israel and undermining all the Torah and the very foundations of the Jewish people. Golias has many claims, which he voices for forty days. He uses all possible arguments, forming theories that are based on facts and logic, and that degrade and negate the Jewish forces, the battalions of the Living God. Scripture reveals that at first there was no fear in the camp of Israel, as it is written: "And they lined up for war against the Philistines" (ibid. v. 2). It was only the words of Golias the Philistine that instilled fear into the heart of the king and the people: "Sha'ul and all Israel heard these words of the Philistine, and they became terror-stricken and greatly afraid" (ibid. v. 11). His words were as firm as his armor. No human rationale could best him in debate, nor could human strength stand up to him in battle. His victory seemed assured.

Against all sound reasoning, common sense, and physical odds, David goes forth, girded with a strength that is beyond logic and deliberation. Against the truth of reality, he goes out with a prophetic truth, the truth of the people of Israel: "You come to me with sword and spear and javelin; but I come to you in the Name of the Eternal, Lord of Hosts, the God of the ranks of Israel that you have ridiculed" (ibid. v. 45). Golias goes on in the way of Orpah; his ego can be seen through his nice words: I am the Philistine who has won battle X and battle Y. David, however, is above any personal ambition, as was Ruth his ancestress, clinging completely to the Creator. Golias holds his ground for forty days, terrorizing Israel, until David defeats him.

Chazal inform us that this entire episode is based on the conflict between the ways of Orpah and Ruth, respectively: "R' Berechia said in the name of R' Yitzchak, 'The forty steps which Orpah took to accompany her mother-in-law delayed her son [Golias' downfall] for forty days' " (*Ruth Rabbah* 2:21). The Gemara cites another of R' Yitzchak's remarks: "May the sons of the one who kissed come and fall by the hand of the sons of the one who held fast" (*Sotah* 42b). The forty days during which Israel was terrorized by Golias were days of the temporary victory of Orpah's course. Ultimately, however, Ruth's outlook prevailed, and the sons of the kissed fell into the hands of the one who clung.

೮೩   ೮೩   ೮೩

The battle of David and Golias is not an isolated phenomenon in the history of the Jewish people; it merely reflects the intense battle that has been raging between the nations of the world and the Jewish people throughout our history. It has served as an eternal example. Whenever Israel went out to battle, the Priest Anointed for Battle would say to them: "They come [relying] on the might of flesh and blood, but you come [relying] on God's might. The Philistines came [relying] on the might of Golias; but what was his fate? He fell by the sword" (*Sotah* 42a). We have been unceasingly provoked by the spirit of Golias the Philistine, which is always accompanied by might, logic, and superficial truth. Earnest truth, however, is expressed in [David's] *Sefer Tehillim*, and it is from this truth that Israel has drawn its power of endurance. What else can explain Rabbi Yochanan ben Zakkai's logic in asking for Yavneh and its sages? What is the rationale for Jewish obstinacy against Greece and its wisdom, or Rome and its power, before both of which the entire world succumbed? Israel's standing among the nations is not deter-

mined by logic, but by adherence: "But you, who adhere
to the Eternal, your God, are all living today" (*Devarim* 4:4).

ogs　ogs　ogs

Upon examination, it is apparent that the very foundation
of the Jewish people defies logic. Chazal relate that the Holy
One, blessed is He, offered His Torah to every nation, but
they all asked, "What is written in it?" Upon hearing what the
Torah demands of man, they rejected it, because it does not
conform to human nature, but rather restrains it. The Jewish
nation alone felt that it had within itself the underlying
strength to overcome man's instincts and said, "We will carry
out and heed." Were it not for this strength, exhibited by
Israel as overriding the truth of human logic, there would
have been no hope for the world's ever attaining its
rectification. However, since the Torah was accepted by Israel,
there is hope that after many ups and downs the whole world
will become aware of the truth, as the prophet has predicted:
**"For just as rain and snow come down from heaven and do
not return there, but rather they irrigate the earth and make
it germinate and grow [vegetation], and they produce seed
for him who sows, and food for him who eats, so is My word
that comes forth from My mouth — it does not return to Me
without effect, but only if it carried out what I desired, and
was successful in what I sent it [to do]"** (*Yeshayahu* 55:10–11).
The world will be irrigated with Godly truth, which will
finally sprout the prophetic messianic vision.

(טו) וַתֹּאמֶר הִנֵּה שָׁבָה יְבִמְתֵּךְ אֶל־עַמָּהּ וְאֶל־אֱלֹהֶיהָ שׁוּבִי אַחֲרֵי
יְבִמְתֵּךְ: (טז) וַתֹּאמֶר רוּת אַל־תִּפְגְּעִי־בִי לְעָזְבֵךְ לָשׁוּב מֵאַחֲרָיִךְ
כִּי אֶל־אֲשֶׁר תֵּלְכִי אֵלֵךְ וּבַאֲשֶׁר תָּלִינִי אָלִין עַמֵּךְ עַמִּי וֵאלֹהַיִךְ
אֱלֹהָי: (יז) בַּאֲשֶׁר תָּמוּתִי אָמוּת וְשָׁם אֶקָּבֵר כֹּה יַעֲשֶׂה יְהוָה לִי
וְכֹה יוֹסִיף כִּי הַמָּוֶת יַפְרִיד בֵּינִי וּבֵינֵךְ: (יח) וַתֵּרֶא כִּי־מִתְאַמֶּצֶת
הִיא לָלֶכֶת אִתָּהּ וַתֶּחְדַּל לְדַבֵּר אֵלֶיהָ:

(15) *[Naomi] then said [to Ruth], "Look! Your sister-in-law has returned to her people and her gods. Go, follow your sister-in-law."* (16) *Ruth replied, "Do not press me to leave you, to turn back from following you, for where you go, I will go, and where you sleep, I will sleep; your people is my people, and your God is my God.* (17) *Where you die, I will die, and there I will be buried. Let the Eternal treat me like this, and even worse, if anything but death separates between me and you."* (18) *[Naomi] saw that [Ruth] was insistent on going with her, so she stopped speaking to her [about it].*

15. [Naomi] then said [to Ruth], "Look! Your sister-in-law has returned to her people and her gods..."

The expression, "Look!...[she] has returned," implies that Naomi was surprised by Orpah's returning, and having seen that, she became worried that perhaps Ruth, too, was not following her wholeheartedly. She therefore pleads with her once again to go back.

One might ask: How did she know that Orpah had also returned to her gods? Chazal pointed out in the Midrash (*Ruth Rabbah* 2:22) that "since she had returned to her people, she had returned to her gods." Similarly, the Targum explained above (v. 10): "For we will return with you to your people — to convert." Joining the Jewish people means believing in God and keeping the commandments. One cannot attach oneself to the Jewish nation without clinging also to God's Torah. In Naomi's daughters-in-law's words, "for we will return with you to your people," was the implication that they would convert. And now that Orpah had returned to her people, she must have also returned to her gods.

16. – 17. Ruth replied, "Do not press me to leave you..."

According to our Sages (see *Ruth Rabbah* 2:23), Ruth's statement consists of two parts. First she expresses her courageous decision that nothing can deter her from going with Naomi, and then she asks Naomi to stop pushing her away, for she would be hurting herself by doing so: "Do not press me" [*Al tifge'i bi* may also be read as *Al tipag'i bi*, meaning:] — do not bring harm upon yourself because of me.

From here on, Naomi's words assume a different character. She begins to prepare Ruth for a new life under the wings of the Shechinah. She lays out before her the controls and restrictions the Torah places upon man, and Ruth replies to every one of Naomi's statements. In the words of our Sages (*Ruth Rabbah* 2:23–24): "Upon hearing this, Naomi began pointing out the laws pertaining to proselytes. She said to her, 'My daughter, daughters of Israel do not go to heathen theaters and circuses.' She replied, 'Where you go, I will go....'"

"AND HAS NOT SAT IN THE
ASSEMBLY OF SCOFFERS"

It is remarkable that according to Chazal's description, Naomi begins the laws pertaining to proselytes not with essential Torah laws — that is, some of the 613 positive and negative Commandments — but rather with side issues, such as refraining from going to the theater or circus. This indicates that she considered this as a prerequisite to accepting upon oneself the yoke of Heaven. One may wonder and ask why this is so. Chazal's words, however — as the words of the Torah — are sometimes scanty and at other times abundant. The Gemara (*Avodah Zarah* 18b) refers to all these places of entertainment as "the assembly of scoffers," of which it is written: "[who] has not sat in the assembly of scoffers; but only in the Torah of the Eternal is his desire..." (*Tehillim* 1:1–2).

From these words in Tehillim we see that scornfulness and the Torah are mutually exclusive. We know that the Torah of God is both a way of life and a complete philosophy of life. The above implies that scornfulness, too, purports to be an acceptable style and system; otherwise, the parallelism is incongruous. Indeed, the Sages comment on the serpent's statement, "And you will become like God knowing [how to distinguish between] good and evil": "From this we see that it [the serpent] was a scoffer" (*Midrash Shocher Tov*). It is obvious that the serpent's words of incitement against God contained a certain outlook — though its nature is unclear to us — which served as mankind's first stumbling block. This shows that scornfulness is not based solely on funny statements, but may even consist of profound principles. Since they do not comply with the truth, however, they are merely mockery. Scoffers should not be characterized as witty or humorous, but as errant and deceitful. That is why the class of scoffers is enumerated among the four classes that will not receive the presence of the Shechinah (*Sotah* 42a). It is for that reason that the passage in Tehillim juxtaposes God's Torah to an assembly of scoffers.

Let us return to the matter of theaters and circuses. We do not know when people began using them or what purpose they served. From the words of our Sages, however, it is clear that they were not merely places of entertainment; rather, their function was to educate man and to guide him in the ways of life. If they were criticized so severely as representing mere mockery, today's reality can certainly justify such criticism. How many flowery words, for instance, have been uttered and repeated concerning using various kinds of "theaters" as, so to speak, humanitarian temples for education and character refinement? And not only have they not helped, but they have even served as agents for stimulating all kinds of evil allurements. For there is neither understanding nor wisdom in potions concocted by quacks intending to perfect mankind!

When Naomi set out to instruct Ruth in the way of Judaism, she first had to uproot all the foundations and concepts she had inherited from Mo'av. So her first lesson to her was: My daughter, know that our entire perception of life differs from that of the gentiles. The daughters of Israel do not search for truth and beauty in theaters and circuses, because in our view they contain only falsehood and impurity. And what the Book of Ruth began, the Book of Tehillim finished: "Fortunate is the man who has not walked...and has not sat in the assembly of scoffers; but only in the Torah of the Eternal is his desire...." We have one way, the Torah, and it alone can pave the course of life and educate man as to what is good for him.

(יט) וַתֵּלַכְנָה שְׁתֵּיהֶם עַד־בּוֹאָנָה בֵּית לָחֶם וַיְהִי כְּבוֹאָנָה בֵּית לֶחֶם וַתֵּהֹם כָּל־הָעִיר עֲלֵיהֶן וַתֹּאמַרְנָה הֲזֹאת נָעֳמִי: (כ) וַתֹּאמֶר אֲלֵיהֶן אַל־תִּקְרֶאנָה לִי נָעֳמִי קְרֶאןָ לִי מָרָא (א במקום ה) כִּי־הֵמַר שַׁדַּי לִי מְאֹד: (כא) אֲנִי מְלֵאָה הָלַכְתִּי וְרֵיקָם הֱשִׁיבַנִי יְהֹוָה לָמָּה תִקְרֶאנָה לִי נָעֳמִי וַיהֹוָה עָנָה בִי וְשַׁדַּי הֵרַע־לִי:

(19) *They both went on until they came to Beis Lechem. When they came to Beis Lechem, the entire city was in turmoil about them and said, "Is that Naomi?!"* (20) *She answered them, "Do not call me Naomi (pleasantness)! Call me Marah (bitterness), for the All-sufficing God has made things very bitter for me.* (21) *I left full [of possessions], and the Eternal brought me back empty-handed. Why do you call me Naomi, when the Eternal has borne witness against me, and the All-sufficing God has made things bad for me?"*

19. They both went on until they came to Beis Lechem.

Rabbi Yehudah bar Rabbi Simon said: "Come and see how dear are proselytes before God. When she decided to convert, the Torah compared her to Naomi, as it is written, 'They both went on' " (*Ruth Rabbah* 3:5). It is marvellous to see how the Sages scrutinized the words of the Prophets. Since the writer of the Megillah included both of them in the word שתיהם ["They both"], it is a sign that they were both equal. But how could they be compared if Naomi was born to an aristocratic Jewish family, while Ruth was a Mo'avi woman? Nevertheless, once she had sincerely made up her mind to convert, she became so endeared as to become elevated to the degree of the most distinguished among the daughters of Israel.

The entire city was in turmoil about them — About both of them. Both women stirred up great excitement with their appearance, each in her own capacity. Apparently, Ruth's coming to the Jewish people made a big impression. Even in our own era, in the provinces of Lithuania, the impression made by the conversion of the righteous proselyte of Vilna, Count Potocki — whose name was engraved in awe upon the hearts of the Jewish masses — was still felt a hundred years after the event. It is easy to imagine the great impact of such an occasion, where a Mo'avi princess turned her back on all the comforts of her past and came to join the Jewish people at such a low point in their history, because she had experienced the purity and holiness of a Jewish family and the extraordinary qualities of the mother of that family. With her coming, however, Ruth stirred up new excitement among the Jewish people, and this served as something of an encouragement and a compensation for Elimelech's flight. Ruth's arrival also became a new summons for an improvement in actions and spiritual enhancement, as Chazal said: "Let Ruth, who did not break faith with her mother-in-law, reprove Israel, who rebelled against God" (*Midrash*).

Naomi's return evoked a different kind of excitement, as the Megillah recounts in concise language:

And [they] said, "Is that Naomi?!" — A second Iyov had appeared, in the form of a woman, in the streets of Beis Lechem. No mouth could express the wave of feelings that flooded the hearts of her beholders. Everyone gazed at her silently, shaking their head. Only one cry escaped their mouths: Is that Naomi?!

That truncated remark expressed the intensity of Naomi's tragedy, as well as the profound astonishment and shock felt by the inhabitants of Beis Lechem at the sight of the poor, broken woman who returned to them from the fields of Mo'av. That expression of incredulity embodied the myriads of questions that could have been raised. It may be explained favorably as well as disparagingly. Some of the people intoned it as a justification: See what has befallen that woman who abandoned her country during a time of depression and famine, with no feeling for the suffering of the poor, returning only now when there is plenty. Others, to the contrary, turn their wonderment heavenward, as did Iyov (without his many complaints, however, for they are mere spectators, rather than actual sufferers): "Is that Naomi, who used to lend her jewelry to the women of Beis Lechem? Is that Naomi whose beauty used to outshine gold?" (*Yalkut*) Is this the reward of Naomi, who was pleasing to both God and people? Why has she been so severely punished? Thus, some of the people justified Elimelech's family, or at least Naomi, for having left the land. Naomi, however, replies:

20. Do not call me Naomi (pleasantness)! Call me Marah (bitterness) ...

Those who called me Naomi were mistaken; I am by nature bitter, and God has embittered me rightly and justly. Chazal (*Ruth Rabbah* 3:7) used the following wonderful analogy: Bar Kapparah told of a man who had taken his cow of a common breed to the market place, claiming that it was a farming cow that had been trained to plow straight, fine furrows. People challenged his veracity by pointing out that if it were such an excellent cow, why did it have such welts on its back? Surely, it had to be beaten with a stick and a whip! Thus, said Naomi: "Calamities that have befallen me attest to the fact that I was never Naomi, for if I had been Naomi, I would not have fallen so low; my end proves my beginning."

21. I left full [of possessions], and the Eternal brought me back empty-handed.

Because I left full of possessions, therefore God brought me back empty-handed. I had everything: fame, honor, and riches. My husband was destined for royalty; my sons were aristocrats, and I, myself, had acquired an unrivaled reputation. But then everything disappeared: My husband and sons are buried in a foreign country, and I have been left a forlorn and pitiful woman. When I was full I felt only my own pleasantness, but now I feel also the bitterness of others.

The Eternal has borne witness against me — God has shown me that there is an eye that keeps watch, and that He conducts His world with justice, so that one eats the fruit of one's deeds. These words contain also an element of consolation. Naomi finds solace in the fact that her misfortune has at least taught others a lesson. She therefore requests: Call me Marah, so that I carry out my mission and that my name attest that God is the Righteous One.

Thus Naomi's response serves as her confession and acknowledgment of divine judgment. Whereas Iyov's friends proffered arguments, she put the blame on herself: The fault lies with me! This shows us her high moral stature, a level which Iyov did not reach, and the reason for the great difference between the outcomes of their afflictions. Iyov of the land of Uz regained his former status, but he left the world around him in its previous sorry state. Naomi's suffering, however, provided the world with the "fourth wheel of the Divine Chariot" — David, the Mashiach's forefather — thus, she became the cause of the world's revival!

(כב) וַתָּשָׁב נָעֳמִי וְרוּת הַמּוֹאֲבִיָּה כַלָּתָהּ עִמָּהּ הַשָּׁבָה מִשְּׂדֵי מוֹאָב וְהֵמָּה בָּאוּ בֵּית לֶחֶם בִּתְחִלַּת קְצִיר שְׂעֹרִים:

(22) *Naomi returned with Ruth the Mo'aviyah, her daughter-in-law, who had returned with her from the fields of Mo'av, and they came to Beis Lechem at the beginning of the barley harvest.*

22. Naomi returned with Ruth the Mo'aviyah, her daughter-in-law ...

The wheel has come full circle from the famine in the first verse to the harvest in the closing verse of our chapter. Elimelech's family left during the famine out of narrow-mindedness and selfishness, assimilating in Mo'av and becoming mired there forever. God made that trip the circumstances which drew out Ruth, who embodied the trait of kindness in its purest manifestation. On the strength of that kindness she clung to Naomi, who for that reason remained the sole survivor of Elimelech's family, returning now to her country during the harvest season together with Ruth. Ruth's role among the Jewish people was to become the matriarch of the descendants of Yishai. That is why Scripture introduces her husband-to-be, Bo'az, at the very beginning of the next chapter.

ב (א) וּלְנָעֳמִי מֵידָע (מוֹדַע ק') לְאִישָׁהּ אִישׁ גִּבּוֹר חַיִל מִמִּשְׁפַּחַת אֱלִימֶלֶךְ וּשְׁמוֹ בֹּעַז:

2 (1) *Now, Naomi had a relative through her husband, a man of great prowess, from the family of Elimelech, and his name was Bo'az.*

1. Naomi had a relative...

This chapter begins the second part of the Megillah, which spreads out before us the chain of events that led to Ruth's marriage to Bo'az, who was, according to our Sages' tradition (*Bava Basra* 91a), Ivtzan the Judge, of Beis Lechem (*Shofetim* 12:8–9). It is apparent from the ensuing events, that even following Ruth's arrival to attach herself to God's people, it was still very far-fetched to imagine that a leader of Israel would marry a woman of Mo'av, concerning whom the Torah admonished: "No Ammoni or Mo'avi may enter (marry into) the congregation of the Eternal" (*Devarim* 23:4). Again the prophet reveals to us the hidden hand of God through human deeds, so that what had hitherto been avoided actually takes place.

The chapter begins by stating that Bo'az was מוֹדַע to Elimelech's family, an expression intimating that he was closer than just a relative, as it is stated in *Iyov* (19:14): "Those close to me stay away; my familiar relatives [מְיֻדָּעַי] have forgotten me" (*Midrash Lekach Tov*). Bo'az was related both to Elimelech and to Naomi, as the word מוֹדַע — placed between "Naomi" and "her huband" — implies. As Rashi explains: "Elimelech, Salmon the father of Bo'az, Peloni Almoni

('So-and-so' [see 4:1]), and Naomi's father, were all sons of Nachshon, son of Aminadav."

Until we come to know him by his ways and actions, Scripture characterizes him as "a man of great prowess" — just as "a woman of valor" is an all-embracing title for a woman of lofty attributes and deeds, as illustrated in *Mishlei* (chap. 31), so is "a man of great prowess" one of the most notable Biblical titles for an admirable man.

The significance of this title is explained in the Torah. When Yisro advised Moshe Rabbeinu to choose men who are worthy of being Israel's judges, he said to him: "And you shall prophetically select, from [among] the entire people, men of great prowess who are God-fearing, men of integrity who despise monetary gain" (*Shemos* 18:21). The Torah then affirms that Moshe "did everything that [Yisro] had said" (v. 24). This is immediately followed, however, with only, "Moshe chose men of great prowess," implying that this designation contained all the other virtues enumerated by Yisro, which are merely elaborations on the meaning of "men of great prowess" (see *Ramban* on *Shemos* 18:21 and *Malbim* on Ruth).

In describing Bo'az, Scripture uses a device that it reserves for the greatest persons: "And his name was Bo'az." From their incisive analysis of the Scriptural style, our Sages determined that when the wicked are mentioned, their name is stated immediately — for example, "Golias was his name"; "Naval was his name," etc. but the reverse is true concerning the righteous: "and his name was Kish"; "and his name was Sha'ul"; "and his name was Yishai," etc. (*Ruth Rabbah* 4:5). Chazal were pointing out that when Scripture highlights the phrase "and his name was" in connection with a person, it is underscoring his deeds, whereby he earned his title. The ego of the righteous is not integral to his deeds, for he performs them solely on their merits. Their "name" therefore precedes them. Everything the wicked do, however — even good deeds — they do for their own benefit and honor. Therefore, they come before their "name." "And his name was Bo'az" indicates that he was an exceptional individual, that all his actions flowed from the purity of his soul, without ulterior motives, and that his name preceded him because of his worthy behavior.

This quality of removing all personal and petty considerations was also the primary attribute of Ruth, as we have seen in the first chapter, and as we will see in the following chapters. Thus, she is similarly called by Bo'az "a woman of fortitude" (3:11). As we peruse the rest of the Megillah, we will observe how that title becomes fulfilled in her in all its aspects. Indeed, both of these extraordinary people, Bo'az and Ruth, were similar in description and merit, and from them sprouted forth and grew the ideal man. How telling is the remark of the Midrash (*Ruth Rabbah* 4:4): Said Rabbi Avahu, "When two giants get married, what do they have? Children of great prowess. Who came out of the marriage of Bo'az and Ruth? David." The Midrash then goes on to explain David's titles, as enumerated in the Book of Shemuel (*Shemuel I* 16:18): "...'who knows how to play' — at Scripture; 'a man of great prowess' — in the Mishnah; 'a man of war' — who knows how to engage in the battle of the Torah; 'who is perceptive' — regarding a good deed; 'well-formed'— in Talmud, etc.; 'and the Eternal is with him' — the Halachah is according to him."

Man is continuously in battle against seductions and enticements by the evil inclination, which Shelomo calls "a great king that surrounds a small town" (*Koheles* 9:14). The Torah itself uses in this connection the term "but you can dominate it" (*Bereshis* 4:7), implying a war-like confrontation. Even minor actions can determine the course of momentous events. Just as mountains are made up of tiny grains of sand, great occurrences evolve from little deeds. "The destruction of Betar came through the shaft of a wagon; the destruction of Tur Malka came through a rooster and a hen; the destruction of Jerusalem came through Kamtza and Bar Kamtza" (*Gittin* 55b). Those great destructions began with petty incidents. As the Sages said: "A man should never single out one son among others, for on account of the two sela's weight of silk, which Ya'akov gave Yosef in excess of his other sons, his brothers became jealous of him, and this led to our forefathers' descent into Egypt" (*Shabbos* 10b). Actually, the descent of the Children of Israel into Egypt was pre-ordained, having been revealed to Avraham in the "Covenant Between the Pieces." It was caused, however, by the "fine wool robe." The opposite occurs as well: "Whoever repeats a statement in the name of the person who said it brings redemption to the world, as it is stated, 'Esther then informed the king, in the name of Mordechai' " (*Avos* 6:6). Though Megillas Esther contains a long chain of events that led to the Jews' deliverance, the "repeating of a statement in the name of the person who said it" became an indispensable part of that chain.

It is an important principle that events recorded in Scripture constitute an integral whole, every detail of which plays a decisive role in its entire development, whether for good or for bad. Thus, here the Prophet Shemuel is showing us how a combination of events developed into David's birth. Through apparently insignificant human actions, he raises us to the highest of human perspectives. We must follow Ruth as she gleans in the field of Bo'az, and collect all the small details, in order to perceive the grand results.

We have now reached the section dealing with Ruth's gleanings. Every time we read it and imagine this princess going out to glean as a poor woman, we shudder: Is this what she deserved after all that she had so sincerely sacrificed? Is this the reward for her good deeds? Yet, the prophet gives this story such prominence! Chazal made the following observation: "Why did Scripture record our ancestors' poverty? To inform their descendants that although they were poor, they trusted in their Creator, thereby earning life in both the World-to-Come and in this world." The Midrash connects the same theme to Ya'akov, Moshe, and David. The crucible of affliction is the most reliable test of one's integrity, for such is the power of truth: Nothing can influence it, and it is destined to prevail.

(ב) וַתֹּאמֶר רוּת הַמּוֹאֲבִיָּה אֶל־נָעֳמִי אֵלְכָה־נָּא הַשָּׂדֶה וַאֲלַקֳטָה
בַשִּׁבֳּלִים אַחַר אֲשֶׁר אֶמְצָא־חֵן בְּעֵינָיו וַתֹּאמֶר לָהּ לְכִי בִתִּי:

(2) *Ruth the Mo'aviyah said to Naomi, "Let me go now to the
field [of] one who will regard me favorably, and gather among
the stalks." She answered her, "Go, my daughter."*

**2. Ruth the Mo'aviyah said to Naomi, "Let me go now to the
field [of] one who will regard me favorably, and gather
among the stalks."**

Ruth apparently made up her mind to do that after careful
deliberation, for they had struggled about how to sustain
themselves, discarding all considerations as unfeasible. Chazal
stated in Midrash Zuta regarding the next verse: "Every day
she went and brought just enough to eat for both of them, to
avoid being influenced to bad behavior or having to rely on
others." Thus, Ruth's main worry was that to obtain a loaf of
bread one might act immodestly, as stated in *Mishlei* (6:26).
Therefore, she was exceedingly careful with her behavior. The
following question begs for an answer, however: Why did
they have to search for a source of sustenance, when Naomi
had such a wealthy kinsman as Bo'az, who surely would not
have ignored his distinguished widowed relative? It must
have been because they did not want to be dependent upon
anyone, even a close relative such as Bo'az. This is also
evident from the continuation of the story, where Bo'az had
to act cunningly to enable Ruth to glean a little extra (see v.
16 below), as they were so determined to eschew dependence
even on relatives. Consequently, Naomi and Ruth decided to
sustain themselves from the gleanings of the poor, which is a
divine gift, rather than accept charity from human hands.
This is in keeping with the well-known saying: "Said the dove
to the Holy One, blessed is He, 'Master of the Universe! May
my sustenance be as bitter as the olive, but under Your
control, rather than sweet as honey, but controlled by flesh
and blood' " (*Sanhedrin* 108b).

This clarifies for us the Torah's view that one must avoid

receiving favors from benefactors and generous people, whoever they may be. Similarly, we find in Chazal, concerning the young Levite, Moshe's grandson, who mistakenly thought idolatry was permissible and served Michah's idol: "He said to them: 'I have the following tradition from my grandfather's family: One should always rather hire himself out to idolatry than be dependent on his fellow creatures' " (*Bava Basra* 110a). His understanding of the matter, however, was incorrect, as the Gemara there explains: He thought avodah zarah meant actual idol worship, but it was not so; rather, it meant, work that was strange to him — avodah shezarah lo — (for example, below his dignity [Rashbam]). This demonstrates how deeply rooted was the desire to be free of reliance on others, even to cause the Levite to err and believe that anything — even idolatry — is permitted to preserve one's self-sufficiency, as long as one's heart is not in it (see *Rashbam* ibid.). The prophet here points to this trait in Ruth, who fulfilled the Torah's moral requirements in all her conduct and actions. The prophets even referred to this as a messianic goal: "...in that they will not rely on a man or put their trust in people" (*Michah* 5:6).

There was also a question regarding the gleaning itself: Which one of them should go to glean — Naomi, the elder, or Ruth, the younger, who for reasons of modesty might be endangering herself. After all, immorality pervaded then, as is quite evident from Bo'az's admonition to the young men (vv. 15–16).

Evidently, the two women deliberated at length. Scripture relates Ruth's decision: Let me go now to the field. She takes it upon herself to go out to the fields to bring food, despite the danger to which she is exposing herself.

We do not know Naomi's reasons for agreeing to it; she surely weighed the matter scrupulously. It must be that she fully trusted Ruth's chastity and prudence. Lest her actions be misinterpreted as not caring about Ruth's welfare because she is her daughter-in-law, she stresses, "Go, my daughter," as if to say, "my consent is not only that of a mother-in-law, but that of a mother."

Ruth's humble decision to go and glean among the poor served as the first link in the chain of events that gave rise to the prospect of marriage to Bo'az.

(ג) וַתֵּלֶךְ וַתָּבוֹא וַתְּלַקֵּט בַּשָּׂדֶה אַחֲרֵי הַקֹּצְרִים וַיִּקֶר מִקְרֶהָ חֶלְקַת הַשָּׂדֶה לְבֹעַז אֲשֶׁר מִמִּשְׁפַּחַת אֱלִימֶלֶךְ:

(3) *She went and came back, and then [went and] gathered [stalks] in the field, behind the harvesters. By chance it happened to her that the section of the field [where she was gathering] belonged to Bo'az, who was from the family of Elimelech.*

3. She went and came back, and then [went and] gathered [stalks] in the field, behind the harvesters.

Chazal focus on the word "וַתָּבוֹא" ("and came back"), which seems to be superfluous, explaining: "She went about marking the trails" (*Ruth Rabbah* 4:6). Rashi explains that she made marks and signs before entering the field, and went and came back to the city, so as not to get lost on the way. "She went and came back," is thus an actual description of how she went. Scripture also describes how she gleaned: "She gathered [stalks] in the field," only the amount that conforms to "gleaning" — "two stalks she gleaned; three stalks she did not glean" (*Shabbos* 113b). Behind the harvesters — She constantly tried to remain out of their sight: "All [other] women chatted while they gathered, whereas she sat and gleaned; all the others flirted with the male reapers, while she concealed herself" (*Ruth Rabbah* 4:8). It was this behavior of hers that caused Bo'az to ask, "Whose young girl is this?"

By chance it happened to her that the section of the field [where she was gathering] belonged to Bo'az — There is well-known saying of Chazal: "No one hurts his finger here on earth unless it was so decreed against him in heaven"

(*Chullin* 7b). In other words, nothing happens by accident; rather, there is a Hand that leads man to the occurrence, or the incident to man. How much more so is this true concerning such momentous events as the birth of important people who affect the destiny of humanity! Regarding the expression, "By chance it happened," in this verse, our Sages say: "It comes to teach us that an angel directed her, similar to the statement, 'God chanced upon Bil'am' " (*Midrash Lekach Tov*). "Accidents" are performed by angels (messengers of God); that is, happenstance in Biblical parlance implies Providential intervention to bring about an indispensable event, whose occurrence in the natural way requires much time and a long chain of intermediate links. It is therefore akin to miraculous when the normal chain suddenly becomes condensed by a Providential development. This may be seen in the prayer of Avraham's servant, Eliezer: "Please arrange [events] before me today" (*Bereshis* 24:12) — Please cause something to happen that will cause me to quickly find, today, the girl that is destined for Yitzchak. The Megillah here points out several incidents that dovetailed, thus shortening the great distance that existed between Ruth the Mo'aviyah and Bo'az the Judge.The first incident was that of Ruth, who immediately appeared in Bo'az's field, and the second was that of Bo'az, as related in the following verse:

(ד) וְהִנֵּה־בֹעַז בָּא מִבֵּית לֶחֶם וַיֹּאמֶר לַקּוֹצְרִים יְהֹוָה עִמָּכֶם וַיֹּאמְרוּ לוֹ יְבָרֶכְךָ יְהֹוָה: (ה) וַיֹּאמֶר בֹּעַז לְנַעֲרוֹ הַנִּצָּב עַל־הַקּוֹצְרִים לְמִי הַנַּעֲרָה הַזֹּאת:

(4) *Just then* [והנה], *Bo'az was coming from Beis Lechem, and he said to the harvesters, "May the Eternal be with you." They answered him, "May the Eternal bless you."* (5) *Bo'az then asked his lad who was in charge of the harvesters, "Whose young girl is this?"*

4. Just then, Bo'az was coming from Beis Lechem...

The word והנה (lit. "behold") is commonly used to emphasize a novelty. Apparently, it was unusual for Bo'az to come to his field during the harvest. Just then, however, he was coming, a fact that led to his meeting Ruth. If not for this meeting, and his taking notice of Ruth's qualities, Naomi would not have been able to make her upcoming proposal.

"GREETINGS SHOULD BE GIVEN IN [GOD'S] NAME"

And he said to the harvesters, "May the Eternal be with you." They answered him, "May the Eternal bless you" — It goes without saying that descriptions depicted in our Megillah are not mere embellishments; rather, they are integrated into the narrative as necessary elements thereof. Therefore, this passage is not merely recounting a detail of how people lived in those days, of how the owner of a field and his workers exchanged greetings. Chazal have explained in the Mishnah, *baraisa* (*Berachos* 54a, 63a), and Midrash (*Ruth Rabbah* 4:7), that, on the contrary, Scripture is here pointing out a great innovation that was then instituted in Israel by Bo'az and his court: that people should greet one another in God's Name.

We, who have everything already laid out for us — in the words of the Yerushalmi, Shekalim: "Our ancestors have already plowed, planted, cultivated, and harvested for us" — can hardly grasp the significance of the innovation in that short greeting. Chazal, however, determined that this was one of the three things decreed by the earthly court that were confirmed by the heavenly court, as the angel said to Gideon: "The Eternal is with you, O mighty hero" (*Shofetim* 6:12). Of all the ordinances established in Israel, this one by Bo'az needed heavenly approval, because it implies a new perception of man and of the relationship between him and his Master. For it is, so to speak, as if we were reducing the Creator and bringing Him down from His heavenly abode to man's domain. In truth, however, it is not debasing to God's glory; it is rather an enhancement of man's, as it is written: "And Your humility made me great" (*Tehillim* 18:36).

Furthermore, the Holy One, blessed is He, seeks, so to speak, a place for Himself in our world, because "the main dwelling place of the Shechinah is on earth" (*Chazal*).

We know from our Sages that this outlook pervades the entire Torah. For example, the Holy One, Himself, blessed is He, served as Adam's "best man" and brought Chavah to him. Additionally, "The Eternal, the All-powerful, made clothes of skin for man and his wife, and [thus] He dressed them" (*Bereshis* 3:21). Similarly, He visited Avraham when he was ill, comforted Ya'akov in mourning, and buried Moshe. As Chazal said: "The Torah begins with an act of kindness and ends with an act of kindness" (*Sotah* 14a). Furthermore, from the Torah's account of Avraham asking God to wait while he received his guests, our Sages learned that "hospitality takes precedence over greeting the Shechinah." Likewise, they taught concerning erasing the parchment containing the Sotah: "For the purpose of establishing harmony between husband and wife, the Torah said, 'Let My name that was written in sanctity be blotted out by the water' " (*Sukkah* 53b). Thus, the entire Torah teaches us the importance of man in the eyes of God, how He looks after his welfare, and is involved, so to speak, in all human affairs. All this is obvious and clear to us today. But who is aware of how much effort the prophets had to invest in plowing and cultivating among the Jewish people in order to plant these truths in them — that is, that respecting man is also respecting God, because man is God's image in Creation, so that God is honored by man's being honored. As our Sages said in Avos: "Who is honored? He who honors others, as it is stated: 'For those who honor Me I will honor, and those who despise Me shall be held in contempt.' "

Bo'az and his judicial forum were the first to introduce this view into the behavior of Israel, as they decreed to include God's name in greetings, and to bless man's handiwork in God's name. The decree must have been appropriate for that particular time, aimed at repairing breaches in Jewish society and healing contemporary ailments, the exact nature of which we do not know. In any event, this was contrary to Elimelech, who despaired of the Jewish people and abandoned them. Here the leaders of the generation took counsel regarding how to bring the Jewish people back to their roots, and to educate and guide them daily in the spirit of Torah. The methods the leaders of Israel chose are remarkable. The new decree was made in order to give a boost to man's lowered honor, and to highlight and purify the image of God in him. The wording of the greeting, "May the Eternal be with you," constitutes not only a blessing, but also a declaration that God dwells among the people. This implies that his dwelling places and actions must be pure, for only then will man deserve to be likened to His Creator.

This common greeting also underscores the equality of all humanity, for we all have one Father, and we have all been created in His image and likeness. Hence, we must honor and act kindly to one another.

Thus, this notable reform instilled in the Jewish people a new attitude in the spirit of Torah, in love for one's fellow, and in acknowledging everyone's importance and merit. This is also the aim of the Book of Ruth, the total essence of which comes to teach us the great virtue of kindness, which is in turn based on recognizing the significance of the human being. The entire foundation of the kingdom of the House of David and the kingdom of the Mashiach rests on the supports of this decree. Were it not for the spirit of this edict, who is to say whether it would have been possible for the judge to converse with the gentile girl, to say nothing of marrying her, for such a step required the laying of much groundwork. The people, too, would have opposed it, if not for the great change, whereby they were being educated about the verities of the significance of man and the purpose of creation. This led to their being ready to acknowledge good deeds from any source, even from a member of another nation. The decree, then, became integrated into the Megillah, because it was one of the things that influenced the final result. It, too, is alluded to in the word וְהִנֵּה, meaning: Behold, Bo'az was coming from a meeting of the Sanhedrin with a new regulation, and that is what led to the events that followed. All this is merely hinted at in the text, because the rule's influence was not apparent.

5. Whose young girl is this?

Bo'az's question was due only to her actions, as described in Verse 3. As Chazal point out: "Was it then Bo'az's practice to inquire about young women?" (*Shabbos* 113b). It was because he had seen her fine qualities, as explained above.

Let us imagine the scene: Bo'az had just arrived from a meeting of the Sanhedrin, which had dealt with the generation's decline and of the blurring of God's image in man, when, lo and behold, he sees a totally unexpected sight: A poor girl is gleaning in the field, displaying diligence, modesty, and wisdom (Torah wisdom — keeping distant from theft). He is curious to find out who the anonymous girl is who is actualizing on her own the lofty traits which hovered before the eyes of the generation's leaders.

(ו) וַיַּעַן הַנַּעַר הַנִּצָּב עַל־הַקּוֹצְרִים וַיֹּאמַר נַעֲרָה מוֹאֲבִיָּה הִיא הַשָּׁבָה עִם־נָעֳמִי מִשְּׂדֵי מוֹאָב: (ז) וַתֹּאמֶר אֲלַקֳטָה־נָּא וְאָסַפְתִּי בָעֳמָרִים אַחֲרֵי הַקּוֹצְרִים וַתָּבוֹא וַתַּעֲמוֹד מֵאָז הַבֹּקֶר וְעַד־עַתָּה זֶה שִׁבְתָּהּ הַבַּיִת מְעָט:

(6) *The lad who was in charge of the harvesters responded, [saying,] "She is a Mo'avi girl who returned with Naomi from the fields of Mo'av. (7) She said [to herself], 'I shall now gather [stalks] and collect among the sheaves, behind the harvesters,' and she came and stood [here] from before morning until now. She has [only] been sitting in the hut now for a short while."*

6.-7. The lad who was in charge of the harvesters responded...

The one in charge of the harvesters responds somewhat at length. Commentators found it difficult to determine whether his words were said in praise, or disapproval, of Ruth (see

especially *Alshich*). Chazal, however, detected in his response
a request of Bo'az: "He said to him: 'Act favorably toward her,
so that she will glean after us' " (*Midrash Zuta*). In other
words, she is worthy of having the leader of the generation
act kindly toward her. Indeed, his words made much more of
an impression on Bo'az than he could have imagined. Who
knows what Bo'az must have felt upon hearing the words,
"She is a Mo'avi girl who returned with Naomi," words that
embodied the entire tragedy of the House of Elimelech,
Prince of Yehudah, whose daughter-in-law was now gleaning
barley as one of the poor. These words also express the virtue
of Ruth, who had given up glory and fame for the lot of the
poor in the midst of Israel. In fact, Bo'az does begin by
speaking in a most friendly manner, even as one would speak
to one's daughter: "Now, my daughter, listen [to me]." Here
begins a series of Bo'az's conversations with Ruth, which, the
prophet having found it necessary to include them in the
Megillah, attests to their having been uttered for the sake of
heaven, free of any selfish motives. That is why the Sages
deliberated over each statement, and revealed to us the
hidden implications therein.

(ח) וַיֹּאמֶר בֹּעַז אֶל־רוּת הֲלוֹא שָׁמַעַתְּ בִּתִּי אַל־תֵּלְכִי לִלְקֹט
בְּשָׂדֶה אַחֵר וְגַם לֹא תַעֲבוּרִי מִזֶּה וְכֹה תִדְבָּקִין עִם־נַעֲרֹתָי:
(ט) עֵינַיִךְ בַּשָּׂדֶה אֲשֶׁר־יִקְצֹרוּן וְהָלַכְתְּ אַחֲרֵיהֶן הֲלוֹא צִוִּיתִי
אֶת־הַנְּעָרִים לְבִלְתִּי נָגְעֵךְ וְצָמִת וְהָלַכְתְּ אֶל־הַכֵּלִים וְשָׁתִית
מֵאֲשֶׁר יִשְׁאֲבוּן הַנְּעָרִים:

(8) *Bo'az then said to Ruth, "Now, my daughter, listen [to me].
Do not go to gather in another field, and do not even leave here
[at all], but stay here close to my girls.* (9) *Keep your eyes on
the field where they are harvesting and follow them; I have
already instructed the lads not to disturb you. And [if] you are
thirsty, you may go to the [drinking] vessels and drink from
where the lads draw water."*

8. Do not go to gather in another field, and do not even leave here [at all], but stay here close to my girls.

Apparently, Ruth was about to leave his field for some reason, so he first entreats her not to do so; it would be improper, since she had "happened" upon this one. Here we gain insight into Bo'az's astute philosophy that "accidents" are the means by which God sometimes communicates with human beings; an "accident" that serves as a sign to man is as significant as a heavenly voice. Thus, we find in the Torah concerning Eliezer: Following the fulfillment of his prayer, "Please arrange [events] before me" (*Bereshis* 24:12), Lavan and Besuel said to him: "Rivkah is here before you. Take [her] and go, and let her be a wife for your master's son, as the Eternal has spoken" (*Bereshis* 24:51; see Ramban there). In a like manner, Bo'az says to Ruth: If you came here by chance, it is as if Divine Providence ordered, "Go to that particular field." Therefore, do not leave here, and let events unfold according to divine plan.

This is how the Midrash (*Ruth Rabbah* 4:9) interpreted the verse: "Do not go to gather in another field" — "Do not go to gods of others"; "and do not leave here [at all]" — "This is my God and I will build a residence for Him"; "but stay here close to my girls" — "This is a reference to the righteous." In other words, "Do not go to gather in another field," because averting heavenly directional signals ("accidents") is akin to turning away from heavenly truth, as in: "Do not go to gods of others." "Do not leave here," because here is where your house — which will be pleasing to God — will be built, as implied by, "This is my God and I will build a residence for Him." And here you will also find a group of proper young women, my maidens, whom you may befriend (to whom Chazal referred as being among "the righteous").

Thus, although Bo'az was apparently speaking of gleaning, he intended that his words bring her into his inner circle in order to instruct her in the ways of a Jewish daughter. It was this intent that excited Ruth.

(י) וַתִּפֹּל֙ עַל־פָּנֶ֔יהָ וַתִּשְׁתַּ֖חוּ אָ֑רְצָה וַתֹּ֣אמֶר אֵלָ֗יו מַדּוּעַ֩ מָצָ֨אתִי
חֵ֤ן בְּעֵינֶ֙יךָ֙ לְהַכִּירֵ֔נִי וְאָנֹכִ֖י נָכְרִיָּֽה׃

(10) *She fell upon her face and prostrated herself on the ground.*
She then said to him, "Why do you regard me favorably by
taking notice of me, when I am a foreigner?"

10. She fell upon her face... when I am a foreigner?

Ruth does not thank him for the permission to glean or to
drink water to her heart's content, which is all Bo'az
apparently granted her, according to the literal meaning of
the text. Rather, she is excited about his warm reaction to her;
that is why she uses the term "[להכירני] taking notice of me,"
which implies a heartfelt concern. Chazal, who discover
hidden implications in the slightest nuances, point out that
she was already subconsciously hinting at some kind of a
familial relationship. It turned out that her premonition was
correct, as they said: "This shows that she was prophesying
that he would marry (להכיר also means 'to know') her" (*Ruth
Rabbah* 5:2). Perhaps the words "I am a foreigner" allude to
that as well, for it would be improper for him to marry a
proselyte. Accordingly, already in their first conversation,
unbeknownst to them, a meeting of the minds was forming.

(יא) וַיַּ֤עַן בֹּ֙עַז֙ וַיֹּ֣אמֶר לָ֔הּ הֻגֵּ֨ד הֻגַּ֜ד לִ֗י כֹּ֤ל אֲשֶׁר־עָשִׂית֙ אֶת־חֲמוֹתֵ֔ךְ
אַחֲרֵ֖י מ֣וֹת אִישֵׁ֑ךְ וַתַּֽעַזְבִ֞י אָבִ֣יךְ וְאִמֵּ֗ךְ וְאֶ֙רֶץ֙ מֽוֹלַדְתֵּ֔ךְ וַתֵּ֣לְכִ֔י
אֶל־עַ֕ם אֲשֶׁ֥ר לֹא־יָדַ֖עַתְּ תְּמ֥וֹל שִׁלְשֽׁוֹם׃ (יב) יְשַׁלֵּ֥ם יְהֹוָ֖ה פׇּעֳלֵ֑ךְ
וּתְהִ֙י מַשְׂכֻּרְתֵּ֜ךְ שְׁלֵמָ֗ה מֵעִ֤ם יְהֹוָה֙ אֱלֹהֵ֣י יִשְׂרָאֵ֔ל אֲשֶׁר־בָּ֖את
לַחֲס֥וֹת תַּֽחַת־כְּנָפָֽיו׃

(11) *Bo'az responded, [saying] to her, "I was repeatedly told*
about everything you did for your mother-in-law after your
husband died, that you left your father and mother and the land
where you were born, and you went to [live among] a nation
that you did not previously know. (12) *May the Eternal repay*
you for your [good] deeds, and may your reward be complete

from the Eternal, God of Yisrael, under Whose wing you have sought protection."

11. Bo'az responded, [saying] to her, "I was repeatedly told."

After hearing her humble words — that she does not know why she merited such attention by him — Bo'az succinctly underscores the significance of her deeds. As our Forefather Avraham had done, she, too, had left her birthplace and father's home for a strange country. Avraham had gone at the command of God and with extensive assurances, yet it was considered as one of the signs of his greatness, a test etched in eternity. Ruth, on the other hand, went due to an inner awakening, with neither hope nor expectation, things which make it easier and lift one's spirits in adversity. Ruth was capable of throwing everything behind her, without demanding any compensation for her sacrifice. And why did she do it all? To bestow kindness upon her mother-in-law, something which does not often conform with the norms of society (see Mishnah in *Yevamos* 117a), especially following the husband's death. Bo'az continues:

12. May the Eternal repay you for your [good] deeds, and may your reward be complete [sheleimah] from the Eternal...

Bo'az's words, as those of Naomi to Orpah and Ruth above, contain a double blessing. Is it not enough to say, "May the Eternal repay you for your [good] deeds"? Why did he have to add, "and may your reward be complete from the Eternal"? What he meant, according to Chazal, was that something extraordinary had to happen in order for her to be repaid. As they explained: "Do not read *sheleimah* [complete or perfect], but Shelomo [Solomon]" (*Yalkut Shimoni* 601). This means, "Your deeds indicate such human perfection that you deserve that the most perfect man should be descended from you, namely, Shelomo." Bo'az then adds a third thing: "under Whose wing you have sought protection." According to our Sages, this is not a reason but a result, as they said in the Midrash (*Ruth Rabbah* 5:4): "Come and see how great is the power of the righteous, and how great is the power of charity [lit. righteousness], and how great is the power of those who perform kindly acts, for they seek protection neither in the shadow of the [wings of] the morning, nor ...of the earth, ...the Chayos, ...the Keruvim, or the Seraphim, but in the shadow of Him Who spoke and the world came into being, as it is stated: "How precious is Your kindness, O God; mankind seeks protection in the shadow of Your wings" (Tehillim 36:8). According to the words of Chazal, the meaning of Bo'az's words is: By your deeds you have raised yourself above the lower as well as the higher worlds, so that you are taking refuge in the shadow of the Throne of Glory.

יג) וַתֹּאמֶר אֶמְצָא־חֵן בְּעֵינֶיךָ אֲדֹנִי כִּי נִחַמְתָּנִי וְכִי דִבַּרְתָּ עַל־לֵב
שִׁפְחָתֶךָ וְאָנֹכִי לֹא אֶהְיֶה כְּאַחַת שִׁפְחֹתֶיךָ:

(13) *She then said, "May you regard me favorably, my lord, for you have comforted me and spoken encouragingly to your maidservant, though I am not even [as worthy] as one of your maidservants."*

13. She then said, "May you regard me favorably, my lord, for you have comforted me..."

Bo'az's statement does not seem to contain words of comfort. Our Sages said: "How did he comfort her? He told her that she would attain prominence, her offspring would be leaders of Israel, and she would wear the royal crown" (Yalkut Shimoni 603). Only Chazal knew what prompted them to use such lofty words and to attribute them to Bo'az. However, it is apparent from Scripture — which provides only the essence of their conversation — that Ruth understood the ramifications of his words and his respect for her, finding comfort for her soul therein. Due to her great humility, though, she does not understand why she deserves such treatment, for in her eyes she is not worthy of being even one of his maidservants — so remarkable was her modesty!

יד) וַיֹּאמֶר לָהּ בֹעַז לְעֵת הָאֹכֶל גֹּשִׁי הֲלֹם וְאָכַלְתְּ מִן־הַלֶּחֶם

וְטָבַלְתְּ פִּתֵּךְ בַּחֹמֶץ וַתֵּשֶׁב מִצַּד הַקֹּצְרִים וַיִּצְבָּט־לָהּ קָלִי וַתֹּאכַל
וַתִּשְׂבַּע וַתֹּתַר:

(14) *Bo'az said to her at mealtime, "Come over here and eat of
the bread, and dip your piece of bread in vinegar." She then sat
at the side of the harvesters and he passed her parched grain,
and she ate and was satisfied and [even] left [some] over.*

14. Bo'az said to her at mealtime, "Come over here..."

According to their literal meaning, these words are not a
continuation of the preceding discussion. It is unrealistic to
assume, however, that Bo'az would listen to her self-effacing
statement without responding. Chazal pointed out that the
word לה [to her] is written without a *mapik* (a dot normally
inserted in the ה), hinting that the meaning might be לא (that
is, that Bo'az meant, "No!"). Through their refined
discernment of linguistic nuances, Chazal felt that the
expression גשי הלם ("Come over here") was unusual: It
contained a tinge of majesty. God uses the term in the
prophetic message to Moshe, "Do not come near [הלם]"
(*Shemos* 3:5), and David uses it when praying before God:
"Who am I...that you have brought me this far [עד הלם]?"
(*Shemuel II* 7:18), meaning, to royalty. Thus, Bo'az's words are
a response to Ruth's self-effacing statement: "God forbid! You
are not [as one] of the maidservants [*amahos*], but [as one] of
the matriarchs [*imahos*]!" (*Ruth Rabbah* 5:5). And so, with royal
courtesy he invites her to share in the humble meal: "Come
over here."

Our Sages state further in the Midrash that when Bo'az
invited her to the meal with expressions of royal honor,
Divine Providence put into his mouth prophetic words
concerning the future royalty that would descend from her:
"Come over here," meaning, "Come near to royalty"; "and eat
of the bread" is a reference to the reigns of Shelomo and
Chizkiyahu; "and dip your piece of bread in vinegar" refers
to [King] Menasheh who sinned (*see Ruth Rabbah* 5:6). It is
possible that just as it is to Ruth's credit that she was the

ancestress of men such as David, Shelomo, and Chizkiyahu,
so is it to her debit that Menasheh was her descendant. The
prophetic words "dip your piece of bread in vinegar" imply
that there is also a slight defect in her. So may we also
understand "Ruth the Mo'aviyah then said" (see below, in v.
21). At any rate, it is apparent that Bo'az's words keep on
rising in quality. At first he mentions nothing concerning
what he knew about her actions. Later, he prefaces his great
admiration with, "I was repeatedly told...." In his third
statement he actually treats her with royal honor. Despite it
all, Ruth becomes neither haughty nor proud. Just as she
reacted to his first words with, "[but] I am a foreigner," and
to his superlative praises with, "I am not even [as worthy] as
one of your maidservants," so after "Come over here" — with
which he virtually presents her with "the glory of majesty" —
Scripture states, "She then sat at the side of the harvesters":
She humbly sat down on the side, as if she were not worthy
of being like them!

**And he passed her parched grain, and she ate and was
satisfied and [even] left [some] over** — The Megillah
recorded the account of that meal for posterity — how he
passed her the food and she ate, etc. — so that it is incumbent
on us to scrutinize that scene, as it has been elucidated by our
Sages. The meal offered to Ruth was clearly insubstantial, as
evidenced by the statement of Chazal: Had Bo'az realized that
Scripture would write concerning him, "and he passed her
parched grain," he would have fed her fattened calves (*Ruth
Rabbah* 5:6). However, a blessing rested upon that humble
meal, which Bo'az had given her with his own hands, surely
in an affectionate and respectful manner, as was his custom
in dealing with everyone, and especially with she who had
deserved his lavish praise. Our Sages assumed that the
blessing could have come in Bo'az's merit, for kindness causes
satisfaction even from a small amount, as the passage "and
whiteness of teeth from milk" (*Bereshis* 49:12) is explained:
Whoever whitens his teeth to his fellow (smiles at him), is
better than one who gives him milk (*Yalkut, Vayechi*). Since it

is written, however, "and she ate and was satisfied and [even] left [some] over," presumably the blessing rested on [the food in] the stomach of that righteous woman (i.e., made her feel sated; *Ruth Rabbah* 5:6).

There are certain ways of comporting oneself while eating. Thus, there is a great difference between how a dignified and respected person eats and how an inferior one does. There are, however, also Torah manners regarding eating, that set apart the spiritually ideal person from one who is flawed — that is, the righteous from the wicked. Chazal refer here to the verse: "The righteous eats to the satisfaction of his soul, but the body of the wicked is never satisfied" (*Mishlei* 13:25). Eating serves the righteous as merely one factor in his content- and significance-laden life. The essence of the wicked person's life, however, is eating and other physical pleasures. Accordingly, the righteous eat to live, whereas the wicked live to eat. The former, therefore, is satisfied by what is needed to survive, while the wicked acts as if his stomach is too limited: "But the body of the wicked is never satisfied" (Gra to *Mishlei*). Similarly, we find in the Torah (in the blessing contained in the second paragraph of the *Shema*): "You will eat and be satisfied" (*Devarim* 11:15) — The genuine blessing is becoming satisfied through eating. The opposite of this is found in the words of the Prophet Chaggai, when, during the ill-fated days of the Second Temple, he refers to a situation of "eating without being satisfied" (*Chaggai* 1:6). Our Sages found in this verse in Megillas Ruth a concrete description of "The righteous eats to the satisfaction of his soul": "And she ate and was satisfied and [even] left [some] over" — Ruth, who personifies human perfection in all her behavior, eats of the grain as much as she does, is sated even to where she leaves some over, in order that her mother-in-law, too, may delight in some of the good food. The words, "and she ate and was satisfied and [even] left [some] over," contain an entire outlook.

(טו) וַתָּקָם לְלַקֵּט וַיְצַו בֹּעַז אֶת־נְעָרָיו לֵאמֹר גַּם בֵּין הָעֳמָרִים

תְּלַקֵּט וְלֹא תַכְלִימוּהָ: (טז)וְגַם שֹׁל־תָּשֹׁלּוּ לָהּ מִן־הַצְּבָתִים וַעֲזַבְתֶּם
וְלִקְּטָה וְלֹא תִגְעֲרוּ־בָהּ:

(15) *She then rose to gather [stalks], and Bo'az ordered his lads,
saying, "Let her also gather between the sheaves and do not
shame her.* (16) *And also [pretend to] forget some of the small
sheaves for her; and you shall leave [them so that] she may
gather [them], and do not criticize her."*

15. She then rose to gather...

The prophet shifts us from one scene to another, affording
us a penetrating look into Ruth's inner soul. We see how all
the honor and praise heaped upon her before all the
bystanders had no effect on her character and behavior: She
bends down again to gather a few stalks. Compare the
wording here to, "She arose while it was still night" (*Mishlei*
31:15), which describes the alacrity of the Woman of Valor.
Fantasies did not hinder her; she rather returned to her
gleaning with renewed zeal.

And Bo'az ordered his lads..."and do not shame her" — It is
apparent that, then as now, people did not give much respect
to the poor. That is why Bo'az had to warn his lads several
times not to cause her humiliation.

16. And also [pretend to] forget some of the small sheaves for her.

We have already commented on the meaning of this verse
above. Ruth was so reluctant to accept gifts that Bo'az found
it extremely difficult to present her with a little of his crop. He
therefore resorted to the ruse of ordering his lads to leave
behind some sheaves, which would appear to have been
"forgotten," hence belonging to the poor.

(יז)וַתְּלַקֵּט בַּשָּׂדֶה עַד־הָעָרֶב וַתַּחְבֹּט אֵת אֲשֶׁר־לִקֵּטָה וַיְהִי כְּאֵיפָה
שְׂעֹרִים: (יח) וַתִּשָּׂא וַתָּבוֹא הָעִיר וַתֵּרֶא חֲמוֹתָהּ אֵת אֲשֶׁר־לִקֵּטָה
וַתּוֹצֵא וַתִּתֶּן־לָהּ אֵת אֲשֶׁר־הוֹתִרָה מִשָּׂבְעָהּ:

(17) *She gathered in the field until evening. She then threshed what she had gathered, and it was an eifah-measure of barley.* (18) *She carried [it] and came to the city, and her mother-in-law saw what she had gathered. She took out and gave her what she had left over after eating her fill.*

17. She gathered in the field until evening.

This again emphasizes her diligence at work, as it is written: "Man goes forth to his work and to his labor until the evening" (*Tehillim* 104:23).

18. She carried [it] and came to the city.

Here, too (as in v. 3), our Sages noted that the words "and came" seem superfluous. Hence they said: "This comes to teach that she did not stop anywhere, to avoid meeting indecent men (*Midrash Lekach Tov*). Notice how our Sages analyzed every letter and nuance to penetrate into their most refined meaning!

And her mother-in-law saw what she had gathered —
Kind-hearted Naomi saw not only the net grain that Ruth had brought, but also "what she had gathered" — she saw how hard Ruth had worked to gather and thresh that which she had ultimately brought.

She took out and gave her what she had left over after eating her fill — She did this quietly and without reservation, expecting nothing in return for having taken the trouble to save and bring a portion to Naomi. She is also not at all enthusiastic to tell about her success and the great and secret things she heard from Bo'az. Had Naomi not coaxed it out of her with questions, Ruth would have kept silent about Bo'az taking notice of her.

(יט) וַתֹּאמֶר לָהּ חֲמוֹתָהּ אֵיפֹה לִקַּטְתְּ (י׳ נוסף) הַיּוֹם וְאָנָה עָשִׂית יְהִי מַכִּירֵךְ בָּרוּךְ וַתַּגֵּד לַחֲמוֹתָהּ אֵת אֲשֶׁר־עָשְׂתָה עִמּוֹ וַתֹּאמֶר שֵׁם הָאִישׁ אֲשֶׁר עָשִׂיתִי עִמּוֹ הַיּוֹם בֹּעַז: (כ) וַתֹּאמֶר נָעֳמִי לְכַלָּתָהּ בָּרוּךְ הוּא לַיהֹוָה אֲשֶׁר לֹא־עָזַב חַסְדּוֹ אֶת־הַחַיִּים וְאֶת־הַמֵּתִים וַתֹּאמֶר לָהּ נָעֳמִי קָרוֹב לָנוּ הָאִישׁ מִגֹּאֲלֵנוּ הוּא:

(19) *Her mother-in-law asked her, "Where did you gather [grain] today and where did you work? May the one who befriended you be blessed." She told her mother-in-law what she had done for [this man], and said "The name of the man by whom I worked was Bo'az." (20) Naomi said to her daughter-in-law, "He is blessed [by] the Eternal, for he has not failed in his kindness to the living and to the dead." Naomi then said to her, "The man is a relative of ours; he is one of the redeemers of our [property]."*

19. Her mother-in-law asked her, "Where did you gather... May the one who befriended you be blessed."

From the words of Chazal and the commentators it is apparent that Naomi felt uneasy upon seeing the large amount Ruth had gleaned, as well as the parched grain she had brought from the field. She became worried that Ruth had unwittingly met up with indecent men. Thus, she posed two questions: "Where did you gather today and where did you work?" — one about the gleaning and one concerning the grain. Her blessing, "May the one who befriended you be blessed," contains hidden within it also a hope: I wish he who befriended you will be among the blessed and not the cursed, the latter of whom it is stated, "Cursed is he who misleads an undiscerning person," or, "who secretly strikes his fellow man" (*Devarim* 27:18, 24). "Secretly" refers not only to that which is hidden from others, but also to what is not known even by the "fellow man" (or woman, in this case), who does not discern the perpetrator's evil intent. Ruth answers Naomi's questions by innocently stating, in an attempt to remove any suspicion, "The name of the man by whom I worked was Bo'az."

The name of the man by whom I worked — "The tongue is the heart's pen" (*Chovos Ha-Levavos*). The tongue helps to reveal conscious as well as subconscious feelings. From the expression used by the poor, "I worked with the master," we can discern the Sages' attitude toward charity, as they stated: "More than the master of the house does for the poor man,

the poor man does for the householder" (*Ruth Rabbah* 5:9). For
the householder acquires around ten mitzvos for the few
pennies given to the poor man: "Open your hand...you shall
continually give him...you must not feel distressed [when
giving him]," and more. Every mitzvah embodies a positive
trait, such as generosity, concerning which it is stated, "All
you desire cannot compare to it" (*Mishlei* 3:15). It is similar
regarding all other good attributes and traits that are bound
up with the mitzvah of charity. This awareness has been
absorbed into the heart and blood of the Jewish people to the
point where the poor use the terminology, "The name of the
man by whom I worked."

**20. Naomi said to her daughter-in-law, "He is blessed [by]
the Eternal... The man is a relative of ours; he is one of the
redeemers of our [property]."**

Ruth innocently mentions Bo'az's name. Naomi, however,
becomes very excited upon hearing that name, even
interweaving a new implication into her words, that is, that
he is a redeemer.

(כא) וַתֹּאמֶר רוּת הַמּוֹאֲבִיָּה גַּם ׀ כִּי־אָמַר אֵלַי עִם־הַנְּעָרִים אֲשֶׁר־לִי
תִּדְבָּקִין עַד אִם־כִּלּוּ אֵת כָּל־הַקָּצִיר אֲשֶׁר־לִי: (כב) וַתֹּאמֶר נָעֳמִי
אֶל־רוּת כַּלָּתָהּ טוֹב בִּתִּי כִּי תֵצְאִי עִם־נַעֲרוֹתָיו וְלֹא יִפְגְּעוּ־בָךְ
בְּשָׂדֶה אַחֵר: (כג) וַתִּדְבַּק בְּנַעֲרוֹת בֹּעַז לְלַקֵּט עַד־כְּלוֹת קְצִיר־
הַשְּׂעֹרִים וּקְצִיר הַחִטִּים וַתֵּשֶׁב אֶת־חֲמוֹתָהּ:

(21) *Ruth the Mo'aviyah then said, "He even said to me, 'Stay
close to my lads until they have completed my entire harvest.'"*
(22) *Naomi said to Ruth, her daughter-in-law, "It is good, my
daughter, that you go out [to gather] with his girls, [so that
men] do not meet you in another field."* (23) *She joined Bo'az's
girls to gather [stalks] until the end of the barley harvest and
wheat harvest, and [then] stayed [at home] with her
mother-in-law.*

21. Ruth the Mo'aviyah then said, "He even said to me, 'Stay

close to my lads until they have completed my entire harvest.' "

Ruth ignores Naomi's subtle hint. She returns to the subject of the gleaning, happily recounting that she has permission to glean in the field until the end of the harvest, so that she need not seek a new location every day. This fulfilled the ideal she had expressed at the beginning: "Let me go now to the field [of] one who will regard me favorably, and gather among the stalks." This princess is content and happy that she will be able to glean in the same field during the entire harvest season!

Ruth's statement contains a puzzling word. In quoting Bo'az, she substitutes "lads" for "girls." Perhaps she did not accurately catch Bo'az's words. Or she might have mentioned the lads to skillfully divert Naomi's hint about Bo'az being a redeemer. Our Sages, however, comment here as follows: Surely she was a Mo'aviyah, for whereas he had said to her, "Stay here close to my girls," she said, "Stay close to my lads" (*Ruth Rabbah* 5:11). She inadvertently expressed what had been in her subconscious. Accordingly, she deserves to be criticized in spite of all her greatness. This also explains the implication in Bo'az's previous remark: "and dip your piece of bread in vinegar" (see above, v. 14).

23. She joined Bo'az's girls... and [then] stayed [at home] with her mother-in-law.

"In faithfulness" (Chazal). Ruth is no longer alone; she has forged ties of affection and friendship with Bo'az's girls, as understood from the word "joined." She remains with them, however, only while working, after which she immediately returns to stay with her aging mother-in-law. Her attachment to girls her age detracts nothing from her benevolent devotion to her mother-in-law, Naomi. What magnanimity is contained in this modest description which the prophet uses to complete the portrayal of the Mother of Royalty! Man is not to be sought in great deeds, for he is usually revealed through small ones, and that is how the Holy One, blessed is He, tests those who fear Him.

ג (א) וַתֹּאמֶר לָהּ נָעֳמִי חֲמוֹתָהּ בִּתִּי הֲלֹא אֲבַקֶּשׁ־לָךְ מָנוֹחַ אֲשֶׁר
יִיטַב־לָךְ:

3 (1) *Naomi, her mother-in-law, then said to her, "My daughter!
Do I not seek a place of contentment [lit. rest] for you that is
good for you?"*

1. Naomi, her mother-in-law, then said to her, etc.

With Naomi's words, the story of the Megillah leaves the
tranquil course of the preceding chapter and takes a new
route, one that is laden with emotional tension.

Naomi's has not been the guiding hand in all events that
have transpired up to this point. She did not invite Ruth to
follow her to the Land of Yehudah; she even discouraged her
at first, in accordance with the laws concerning proselytes.
Even Ruth's going out to the field, which led to the new chain
of events, was her own idea and not Naomi's. Certain
incidents ("angels," in Midrashic terminology) occurred that
clandestinely brought Ruth and Bo'az together. These
incidents carried out their mission, causing Bo'az to take
special notice of Ruth, and leading to the conversations and
actions recorded in Chapter 2. Needless to say, Naomi had no
part in them at all. However, from all she had heard from
Ruth, Naomi perceived a possibility that she could not have
conceived of previously. The time of her decisive involvement
had now arrived, as our Sages expound on this verse: "She
started thinking that perhaps Bo'az would marry her without
her full consent, therefore she began persuading her"
(*Midrash Zuta*).

No one could estimate and value the full potential benefit
inherent in a match between Bo'az and Ruth, two such
exceptional and exemplary individuals. First of all, it would
be most beneficial to Ruth herself, as Naomi apprises her.
Secondly, it would yet be able to be written about herself, the
barren Naomi, "A son was born to Naomi" (4:17).
Furthermore, it would purge all the past of her family, for it

would be recorded in the writings of the House of Israel: "[I have...acquired for myself] Ruth the Mo'aviyah, the wife of Machlon, as a wife, to perpetuate the name of the deceased on his inherited property, so that the name of the deceased not be obliterated from among his brethren..." (4:10). This would actually resurrect the house of Elimelech! Yet, above and beyond all that had to do with herself and her family, just as Bo'az realized that Ruth was destined for greatness — to become the mother of Jewish royalty — Naomi, too, felt and knew that, as we explained her blessing, above: "May the Eternal grant you that each..." (1:9). See also our explanation of the words of the women in the next chapter. Thus, it is possible that something began to take shape in Bo'az's field that would provide the foundation and support of the building of the Mashiach, redeemer of the Jewish people and of the entire world. This is what aroused Naomi to facilitate the events and bring them to fruition.

According to the Targum, Naomi swore that she would not rest until she had fulfilled her task. We are reminded of David's oath that he would not sleep until he found a place to build the House of God (*Tehillim* 132:2–5). Here we see that also the beginning of the House of David grew from an oath to find a place of rest.

It is very clear that had there been a normal way to accomplish her goal, Naomi would not have presented her daring suggestion, one that jeopardized Bo'az's and Ruth's honor, and perhaps her life as well. For Bo'az later tells her, "So now, my daughter, do not be afraid" (3:11), which is explained by the Sages as implying that "she was afraid they would kill her" (*Midrash*). This means that despite all that was narrated in the second chapter, it was still impossible to speak about it to Bo'az himself — or there were grounds for suspecting that he would refuse, for the same reason as did the anonymous would-be redeemer, who said, "so that I do not ruin [the name of] my descendants" (4:6). Naomi found it necessary to influence Bo'az in an unusual manner, to make him face the fact that he was the redeemer. Apparently, however, Ruth too had not accepted the idea of marrying an old man, with Bo'az himself realizing how great a sacrifice this would entail on her part (3:10). Naomi had to induce Ruth to accept that very idea, as well as to go to the barn — an unnatural step toward an unorthodox goal. She begins with persuading talk about the end, which might be able to justify the means. "She began enticing her with words, to prevent her from saying what was requested of her" (*Midrash Zuta*).

"My daughter! Do I not seek a place of contentment [lit. rest] for you..." — By opening with "my daughter," and repeating the words "for you," Naomi stresses that she is giving advice not to benefit herself, by eternalizing her dead son, but that "I would have suggested it even were you my own daughter, because it will bring you contentment and it is the best thing for you." After positing this supposition, which also meets with the approval of the Megillah's author, she continues, "So now, is not Bo'az," etc.

Regarding the expression, "Do I not seek a place of contentment for you?" — which is similar to what she had first said to Ruth and Orpah, "that each find contentment in her husband's home" (1:9) — our Sages make the following comment: "From this we see that a woman has no contentment except in her husband's home" (*Ruth Rabbah* 2:15). Chazal are teaching us that nothing in the world — neither riches, fame, or royalty — can bring a woman the emotional state called "contentment," something she is able to attain only in her husband's home.

(ב) וְעַתָּה הֲלֹא בֹעַז מֹדַעְתָּנוּ אֲשֶׁר הָיִית אֶת־נַעֲרוֹתָיו הִנֵּה־הוּא זֹרֶה אֶת־גֹּרֶן הַשְּׂעֹרִים הַלָּיְלָה:

(2) *So now, is not Bo'az, with whose girls you were [harvesting], our relative? He is going to be winnowing [his] barn of barley tonight.*

2. He is going to be winnowing [his] barn of barley tonight.

The Book of Ruth reveals to us more about contemporary life than any other Biblical book. It shares with us all the doings of the Megillah's personalities: their goings and comings, their lying down and arising. It is difficult for us to conceptualize how Bo'az, the leader of the people, could lie down at the edge of the heap, watching his grain. The Sages, however, did not view that as something primitive; they rather derived an abiding principle from it: "To the righteous their money is dearer than their body, because they do not stretch out their hand to robbery" (Sotah 12a). Bo'az's behavior teaches us a rule for living: Even the greatest person must guard his property, and nothing need deter him. This is the Torah way, and so did our forefather Ya'akov act at the crossing of the Yabbok ford: After he crossed over his abundant property — as the Torah itself attests by stating, "The man grew exceedingly wealthy" (Bereshis 30:43) — he returned to retrieve some small pitchers (see Rashi to Bereshis 32:25). This teaches us that even in wealth one must be careful with every penny. Chazal also derived this from how Moshe's box was made. The Torah emphasizes that it was made of plain wood, of bulrushes, with no regard for the welfare of the child that was being cast into the water (see Sotah 12a). Even under such conditions and in such a situation, which the human mind cannot imagine, one must think about being frugal, so as not to be tempted to dishonesty.

We cannot reconcile such a narrow view with our perspective, but if we reflect on it we will find that it contains the very foundation for building life and for the world's existence. The Torah has already taught us in the narrative of the Flood that the world and all therein were destroyed because of larceny. The Halachah itself exhorts one who does wrong to his fellow: "He Who punished the generation of the flood and the generation of the dispersion, He will take vengeance on he who does not stand by his word" (Bava Metzia 44a). This is because the path from small injustices to the Flood is a direct one: Every small robbery, as well as every grand larceny, is due to man's not being satisfied with a little, desiring instead to increase his possessions at the expense of others.

This is an all-encompassing outlook — that is, a person should constrain himself and thus avoid being attracted to that which does not belong to him. Were this principle to have been instilled into the fabric of society and people's education, the world would have been spared of all wars, and we would not be witness to all the corruption and predicaments that occur even today. Who can say what life and the world would have then looked like! Thus, regarding Moshe Rabbenu, through whom were given the commandments "You must not steal" and "You must not covet" — to which "You must not murder" is also connected — his very beginning in the world was characterized by the realization of the principle of self-restraint. "Moshe is truth and his Torah is truth," for his Torah was fulfilled in his person.

The prophet paints the same picture for us concerning Bo'az, the Mashiach's ancestor. He did not eat fattened calves, but rather bread in vinegar and parched grain, and he personally guarded his barn, for it is through such simple and frugal living that it is possible to build a just and honest society (see Rambam's *Moreh Nevuchim* III:33).

(ג) וְרָחַצְתְּ ׀ וָסַכְתְּ וְשַׂמְתְּ שִׂמְלֹתֵךְ (שִׂמְלָתֵיךְ ק') עָלַיִךְ וְיָרַדְתִּי (וְיָרַדְתְּ ק') הַגֹּרֶן אַל־תִּוָּדְעִי לָאִישׁ עַד כַּלֹּתוֹ לֶאֱכֹל וְלִשְׁתּוֹת: (ד) וִיהִי בְשָׁכְבוֹ וְיָדַעַתְּ אֶת־הַמָּקוֹם אֲשֶׁר יִשְׁכַּב־שָׁם וּבָאת וְגִלִּית מַרְגְּלֹתָיו וְשָׁכָבְתִּי (וְשָׁכָבְתְּ ק') וְהוּא יַגִּיד לָךְ אֵת אֲשֶׁר תַּעֲשִׂין:

(3) *"So bathe and anoint yourself, put on your [best] clothes, and go down to the barn. Do not, [however,] make yourself known to the man until he finishes eating and drinking. (4) Then, when he lies down, you shall note the place where he is lying, and come and uncover his feet and lie [there]; and he will [then] tell you what you shall do."*

3. So bathe and anoint yourself, put on your [best] clothes, and go down to the barn.

"Bathe — because of the impurity of idolatry; anoint yourself — with mitzvos; put on your [best] clothes — Sabbath clothes; and go down to the barn — this is spelled with an extra yod [וירדתי — as if it were stated, 'and I will go down to the barn,' implying,] 'my merit will accompany you'" (*Ruth Rabbah* 5:12). Naomi was fully aware that such a step required much heavenly assistance, to prevent it from backfiring. She therefore instructed Ruth in many preliminaries, so that her intentions would be altruistic and her actions crowned with success. It was not enough that Ruth had come to take shelter under the wings of the Divine Presence; she required yet more purification. All the kindness she had performed was insufficient; she had to do more good deeds. And despite all this, she was still in need of Naomi's merit, for Naomi's intentions were surely for the sake of Heaven. Rivkah acted similarly when, after ordering Ya'akov to disguise himself as Esav before Yitzchak, she said, "My son, let your curse be upon me" (*Bereshis* 27:13; see also Targum there).

4. You shall note the place where he is lying...

Be careful to find out exactly where he is, because a mistake in this may yield disastrous results.

And he will [then] tell you what you shall do — Naomi herself is unsure of the outcome. She only knows that Bo'az will take note of her situation and find a remedy for it. And that is indeed what happened, as told at the end of the chapter.

The inspired author, Ba'al Ha-Akeidah, analyzed Naomi's advice, which deviates so much from the moral and right way. It would clearly be an unacceptable norm for ordinary people. Such a step could only be taken under very special conditions, and by such great persons regarding whom it is absolutely clear that all they do is motivated by moral law. To properly understand such individuals, we must peel away their outer covering and clothe them in white, as befits such virtuous ones. It is similar to how we understand the Torah narrative about the mandrakes: Everything was worthwhile for our matriarchs that could contribute to the proliferation of children and the building of the House of Israel. Ya'akov himself, when discussing the time of his upcoming wedding to Rachel, expresses himself to Lavan in terms that for others would be characterized as utterly vulgar (*Bereshis* 29:21; see also Rashi there). Since the words emerged from Ya'akov's genuineness and purity of soul, however, they are most sacred. It is also difficult for us to understand how Tamar's deed earned her credit for generations. And note the lavish praise our Sages bestowed on Yehudah's confession, "She is right. [She is pregnant] from me..." (*Bereshis* 38:26), in response to which a heavenly voice proclaimed, "From Me came these secret things," that is, they were divinely inspired.

There is a similarity between Naomi's suggestion and the story of Tamar and Yehudah. Presumably, therefore, Naomi learned something from Tamar. This is strengthened by the fact that in the end everyone agrees with the analogy (see 4:12 below). The chain of events connected to Ruth, including Naomi's recommendation, was guided by Divine Providence, as were events surrounding the deed of Yehudah and Tamar. As Chazal explained the text in *Divrei Ha-Yamim* I 4:22: " 'Yashuvi Lechem' refers to Ruth the Mo'aviyah, who came and attached herself to Beis Lechem; 'and the things are ancient' means that these things were said by the Ancient of days" (i.e., God; *Bava Basra* 91b). Rashi explains: " 'From Me came these secret things' — they are the same things that were said in connection with Tamar."

(ה) וַתֹּאמֶר אֵלֶיהָ כֹּל אֲשֶׁר־תֹּאמְרִי (אֵלַי קרי ולא כתיב) אֶעֱשֶׂה: (ו) וַתֵּרֶד הַגֹּרֶן וַתַּעַשׂ כְּכֹל אֲשֶׁר־צִוַּתָּה חֲמוֹתָהּ:

(5) *She answered her, "Whatever you tell me [to do] I shall do."*
(6) *She then went down to the barn, and did everything her mother-in-law had instructed her [to do].*

5.-6. She answered her, "Whatever you tell me...I shall do."

Our Sages profoundly stress that the word אֵלַי (to me) is pronounced but not written in the text (*Ruth Rabbah* 5:13). The prophet, who wrote the Megillah, left out the word אֵלַי, which expresses Ruth's subjective connection to the situation. Ruth's "me" (self) plays no role in her agreement, for had she listened to her inner self she would not have agreed, for reasons stated above. She was, however, certain that whatever Naomi suggests is divinely inspired and is intended for the sake of Heaven. Hence, Ruth is ready and willing to do whatever she says, even if it against her inclination and nature. The text adds, and [she] did everything her mother-in-law had instructed her [to do] — Everything she did was not motivated by her own feelings, but because she was told to do so by her mother-in-law. As our Sages said: "Let Ruth the proselyte, who did not oppose her mother-in-law, reprove the people of Israel who rebelled against Me, as it is written: 'Woe to them, for they have moved away from Me' " (*Hoshe'a* 7:13). Ruth, who dedicated body and soul to carry out her mother-in-law's command, serves as a model for future generations, from whom the Jewish people must learn a lesson!

(ז) וַיֹּאכַל בֹּעַז וַיֵּשְׁתְּ וַיִּיטַב לִבּוֹ וַיָּבֹא לִשְׁכַּב בִּקְצֵה הָעֲרֵמָה וַתָּבֹא בַלָּט וַתְּגַל מַרְגְּלֹתָיו וַתִּשְׁכָּב: (ח) וַיְהִי בַּחֲצִי הַלַּיְלָה וַיֶּחֱרַד הָאִישׁ וַיִּלָּפֵת וְהִנֵּה אִשָּׁה שֹׁכֶבֶת מַרְגְּלֹתָיו: (ט) וַיֹּאמֶר מִי־אָתְּ וַתֹּאמֶר אָנֹכִי רוּת אֲמָתֶךָ וּפָרַשְׂתָּ כְנָפֶךָ עַל־אֲמָתְךָ כִּי גֹאֵל אָתָּה: (י) וַיֹּאמֶר בְּרוּכָה אַתְּ לַיהֹוָה בִּתִּי הֵיטַבְתְּ חַסְדֵּךְ הָאַחֲרוֹן מִן־הָרִאשׁוֹן לְבִלְתִּי־לֶכֶת אַחֲרֵי הַבַּחוּרִים אִם־דַּל וְאִם־עָשִׁיר:

(7) *Bo'az ate and drank and felt cheerful, and [then] came to lie down at the edge of the [grain] heap. She then came quietly, uncovered his feet and lay down.* (8) *Then, at midnight, the man became terrified and [felt himself] being held tight, and there was a woman lying at his feet.* (9) *He asked [her], "Who are*

*you?" She answered, "I am Ruth, your maidservant, and you
may spread your cloak over your maidservant [in marriage], for
you are a redeemer [of our property]."* (10) *He said [to her],
"You are blessed [by] the Eternal, my daughter! You have
surpassed your first [act of] kindness with your second, by not
going after young men, whether [they be] poor or rich."*

7. Bo'az ate and drank and felt cheerful...

Our Sages' comment on this verse suggests that
sometimes even normal activities, which put one into a
certain frame of mind, become motivators to the performance
of acts that are higher than man's inner nature (see *Ruth
Rabbah* 5:15).

**8.-10. Then, at midnight, the man became terrified and [felt
himself] being held tight.... She answered, "I am Ruth, your
maidservant.... He said [to her], "You are blessed [by] the
Eternal, my daughter!**

Who could describe the spiritual terror embodied in the
words "the man became terrified and [felt himself] being held
tight"? Here the leader of the people — who has been
working constantly on improving the generation's moral
state, even sleeping in his barn because of the widespread
immorality of the times — awakens in the middle of the night
to find a woman sleeping at his feet! How degenerate and
impudent on the woman's part, and what an embarrassment
and temptation for him! The bizarre experience terrified Bo'az
to the core. It would have been natural for him to curse and
chase away this woman who had come to put him to such
shame.

Had he uttered a curse, Ruth would have been totally
rejected as a result of Naomi's suggestion. Yet, the opposite
occurred! Chazal here applied the passage, "Man's fear will
produce a snare, but he who trusts in the Eternal will be
strengthened" (*Mishlei* 29:25). In other words, fear normally
causes one to stumble, but "he who trusts in the Eternal will
be strengthened": In the merit of Ruth's kindness and
Naomi's trust, Divine Providence changed Bo'az's heart for

the good and, instead of cursing, he blessed Ruth! This has been classified as a miracle and listed among the other miracles that occurred at midnight. According to our Sages' interpretation, it was to this that David was alluding when he said: "At midnight I rise to thank You for Your just judgments" (*Tehillim* 119:62). All his life King David arose at midnight and reviewed what had happened to the Jewish people from the beginning of its history: Sarah's rescue from Paroh, then the Exodus from Egypt and all the accompanying miracles, followed generations later by the defeat of Sancheriv at midnight. These were characterized by judgment meted out on the one hand — for example, to Paroh, Egypt, and Sancheriv — and benevolence on the other hand: To our matriarch, Sarah, and to the Jewish people. While thanking God every midnight for these miracles, David remembered to include also the miracle that occurred in his great-grandfather's barn, where instead of applying equitable strict justice, God acted charitably, as the Midrash states: "And for the charitable acts that You performed for my great-grandparents, for if he had impulsively cursed her, whence would I have come? You, however, put it into his heart to bless her." Chazal used the specific term "impulsively" to emphasize Bo'az's unparalleled self-control in a situation where he would have been completely justified in reacting out of panic, having had such a scare. More will be said about this later. His evaluation of Ruth's approaching him was not affected by outward appearances, but by the essential quality of the event, its inherent kindness: You have surpassed your first [act of] kindness with your second.

You have surpassed your first [act of] kindness with your second — The commentators struggled with the "first act of kindness." Rashi explains it as referring to "the kindness she did with the living and the dead." Targum Yonasan says, "The kindness you did by converting" (see *Alshich* and *Iggeres Shemuel*). On the surface level we may ask: What does conversion have to do with kindness? Apparently, however, all Ruth's behavior, including her wish to convert, was motivated by a desire to perform kind deeds. Whereas Yisro, Rachav, and Na'aman all expressed — each according to his or her respective conception — a belief in the God of Israel, Ruth does not do so. Furthermore, Scripture underscores her devotion to Naomi, but omits any reference to her devotion to God. Even when she is actually in the process of converting, telling Naomi, "your people is my people, and your God is my God," her words are aimed mainly at Naomi. Perhaps the kindness inherent in her clinging to Naomi could be seen as clinging to God and His Torah, for God is kindness and His Torah is kindness. In any event, it is evident that her conversion, too, was motivated by the trait of benevolence, and this is the path of the Mashiach.

This may be further explained according to the Sages' comment on the verse, "How beautiful are your steps in [perfectly fitting] shoes, daughter of nobility!" (*Shir Ha-Shirim* 7:2): "This refers to the daughter of our forefather Avraham, who was called 'the noble one' for having been the first of the proselytes" (*Chagigah* 3a). Rashi explains that his generosity moved him to acknowledge his Father in heaven. In other words, Avraham's attribute of kindness led him to recognize the truth. There is a great lesson in this: Through his intellect man cannot attain pure understanding, or attach himself to the Source of Truth, unless his heart is refined and pure; otherwise, his heart hinders him. Consequently, it was Ruth's trait of kindness that brought her to recognize her Father in heaven.

As to the "second kindness," Bo'az himself states it: "by not going after the young men." This contains a profound lesson: Despite Bo'az's great admiration for Ruth's self-sacrifice of giving up a life of comfort to embrace a strange people, he admired her even more for her willingness to entrust her fate to an old man, albeit the leader of his generation, and a wealthy judge. Although her previous concessions also manifested noble-mindedness, her last one lacks any hint of luster; it is rather bound to bring her derision. Nevertheless, she found the spiritual courage for that step as well, in order to raise a name for the deceased. That is why her second kindness is greater than the first.

(יא) וְעַתָּה בִּתִּי אַל־תִּירְאִי כָּל אֲשֶׁר־תֹּאמְרִי אֶעֱשֶׂה־לָּךְ כִּי יוֹדֵעַ כָּל־שַׁעַר עַמִּי כִּי אֵשֶׁת חַיִל אָתְּ:

(11) *"So now, my daughter, do not be afraid. Whatever you say I shall do for you, for all [the elders of] my people [who sit at] the gateway [of the court] are aware that you are a woman of fortitude."*

11. So now, my daughter, do not be afraid.

This verse sheds light on what was going through Ruth's mind. Evidently, after she had apparently implicitly carried out Naomi's instructions, she began worrying about the danger that awaited her: Bo'az is liable to scream out, and the men in the field would assume that she is a loose woman and condemn her. According to Chazal, she was afraid that they might kill her. Bo'az therefore allays her fears by saying, "for all [the elders of] my people [who sit at] the gateway [of the court] are aware that you are a woman of fortitude." Since everyone has already come to the conclusion that she is a woman of valor — that is, that she possesses all the good qualities for which a woman may be proud — they will not suspect her, just as people do not look for flecks on the sun. Indeed, instead of condemning her for coming to Bo'az's barn at night, they will see the positive side of it and applaud her for taking such a courageous step. While "the brazen goes to Gehinnom" (*Avos* 5:24), we are instructed to "be bold as a leopard" (ibid. 5:23); it all depends on who the subject is, how the boldness is carried out, and for what purpose.

Everyone could discern in Ruth's boldness her pure intent for the sake of Heaven, as Bo'az himself recognized, and as the Targum here adds: "You have the power to understand the explicit commands of God." For Ruth said, "Spread your cloak over your maidservant [in marriage], for you are a redeemer [of our property]." She plucked up courage, therefore, only to ask him to fulfill the Torah's command, "His redeemer who is related to him may come" (*Vayikra* 25:25). Ruth demonstrated that no spiritual impediment is strong enough to hamper one from carrying out what he must, as David said: "And I will speak of Your testimonies in the presence of kings, and I will not be ashamed" (*Tehillim* 119:46).

Ruth honed all her skills before approaching Bo'az, including counsel and strength, which are among the six qualities enumerated regarding the Mashiach (*Yeshayahu* 11:2). Bo'az knew that the Jewish people would not tarnish the reputation of this woman of valor.

With these words Bo'az also dissipated Ruth's worry that the people would oppose the judge's marriage to a daughter of Mo'av. Thus, he soothes her with: "for all [the elders of] my people [who sit at] the gateway [of the court] are aware that you are a woman of fortitude" — the people know your character and will not impede the marriage. This is in fact what happened, as is brought down in the following chapter.

(יב) וְעַתָּה כִּי אָמְנָם כִּי אם (אם כתיב ולא קרי) גֹּאֵל אָנֹכִי וְגַם יֵשׁ גֹּאֵל קָרוֹב מִמֶּנִּי: (יג) לִינִי (נ' רבתי) הַלַּיְלָה וְהָיָה בַבֹּקֶר אִם־יִגְאָלֵךְ טוֹב יִגְאָל וְאִם־לֹא יַחְפֹּץ לְגָאֳלֵךְ וּגְאַלְתִּיךְ אָנֹכִי חַי־יְהֹוָה שִׁכְבִי עַד־הַבֹּקֶר: (יד) וַתִּשְׁכַּב מַרְגְּלוֹתָו עַד־הַבֹּקֶר וַתָּקָם בְּטֶרֶם (בְּטֶרֶם ק') יַכִּיר אִישׁ אֶת־רֵעֵהוּ וַיֹּאמֶר אַל־יִוָּדַע כִּי־בָאָה הָאִשָּׁה הַגֹּרֶן:

(12) *"But now, however, though [*אם* — if] I am a redeemer [of your property], there is also a redeemer who is a closer relative than I. (13) Stay [here] tonight, and in the morning, if [the redeemer] redeems you, it is good [that] he redeems you, but if he does not wish to redeem you then I, myself, will redeem you. [I swear to this,] as the Eternal lives. Sleep [here] until morning." (14) She slept at his feet until morning, and rose*

when no one could yet recognize his fellowman, [for Bo'az] said
[to himself], "Let it not be known that the woman came to the
barn."

12.-14. But now, however, though [אִם — if] I am a redeemer...
Stay [here] tonight, and in the morning, if [the redeemer]
redeems you, it is good... and [she] rose when no one could
yet recognize his fellowman, [for Bo'az] said [to himself],
"Let it not be known that the woman came...."
It is utterly clear from all this that Bo'az had already
decided to redeem Ruth, as he had said to her, "Whatever you
say I shall do for you," and as Ruth had already discerned
from his having taken special notice of her, as explained
above. The word אִם (if) is read (but not written in the text)
before "I am a redeemer," because he did not consider himself
(merely as) a conditional redeemer; rather, because it is a
commandment of the Torah that the closest relative takes
precedence (*Kiddushin* 21a), he presented the choice to a
nearer kinsman, as explained in the Midrash.

Apparently, this is how the proceedings between them
ended. It was therefore appropriate that Ruth leave, in order
to preserve Bo'az's reputation and to avoid ungodliness. On
the other hand, could one let Ruth walk alone at night in the
fields, where she is liable to come across bawdy characters? It
was a matter of his honor being weighed against hers —
whose is more important? Evidently, Ruth got up to leave, but
Bo'az — despite worrying about his honor and desecrating
the Name of Heaven — pleads with her: "Stay [here]
tonight... Sleep [here] until morning." He gives everything up
for Ruth's honor! This is similar to what happened with
Tamar (see *Bereshis* 38:25), concerning which our Sages said:
"It is better to cast oneself into a fiery furnace rather than put
one's fellow to shame in public" (*Berachos* 43b). As for Bo'az
himself, all he could do was pray for heavenly mercy, as
Chazal learned from Scripture: All that night Bo'az lay
prostrate upon his face praying: "Master of the Universe, it is
revealed and known to You that I have not touched her. May
it be Your will that it not be known that the woman came to

the barn, that the Name of Heaven not be profaned through me" (*Ruth Rabbah* 7:1).

Our Sages (in *Sanhedrin* 19b), while comparing Yosef's trial with Potiphar's wife to that of Bo'az, found a difference between them: Rabbi Yochanan said, "Yosef's strong [temptation] was a small trial to that of Bo'az." Rashi (there) explains that Bo'az could dismiss it out of hand. The Torah itself refers to Yosef's trial as one that took great moral strength: "He left his garment in her hand, and fled." As the Midrash states: "The sea saw and fled" (*Tehillim* 114:3) — "in the merit of 'He left his garment in her hand, and fled' " (*Bereshis Rabbah* 7:10). Just as the fleeing of the sea was caused by the unleashing of a powerful force to counter its natural state, so was the fleeing of Yosef. This is an exemplary story that shows man's ability to repress his evil inclination. Yosef is held up as an example for all time, in the words of the Gemara concerning one who claims that his drives prevented him from fulfilling his obligations in life: "They would say [to the sensual person], 'Were you harassed by your passions more than Yosef?' " (*Yoma* 35b).

Bo'az's trial was greater than Yosef's (see Rashi to *Sanhedrin* 19b): "[Ruth] was unmarried and in bed with him. [Potiphar's wife] was married, however, and not in bed with Yosef." Scripture mentions Bo'az's trial without fanfare, simply as "something of little significance," in the words of Rashi, for that is how Bo'az, the man of great prowess, acted — modestly and with self-control, as though nothing unusual had occurred. In his heart, however, he was aware of the dangers involved, and that is why he prayed all night. The crown of Bo'az' behavior is described in the next verse:

(טו) וַיֹּאמֶר הָבִי הַמִּטְפַּחַת אֲשֶׁר־עָלַיִךְ וְאֶחֳזִי־בָהּ וַתֹּאחֶז בָּהּ וַיָּמׇד שֵׁשׁ־שְׂעֹרִים וַיָּשֶׁת עָלֶיהָ וַיָּבֹא הָעִיר:

(15) *He said [to her], "Bring the kerchief you are [wearing] and hold it [out]," and she held it [out]. He measured out six barley*

grains and placed [them] upon her, and [then] went to the city.

15. He said [to her], "Bring the kerchief..." He measured out six barley grains...

Morning is near and it is urgent that she go, so that "it not be known." He finds it necessary, however, to delay Ruth because of six barley grains. How he delays, and with such patience and indulgence: Bring the kerchief...and hold it [out]...and she held it [out]... He measured out...and placed [them] upon her. Is he not worried lest someone see and people begin complaining about his paying a prostitute before daybreak? Of course he is worried, but he is willing to take that risk in order to accomplish the objective that he considers as very important. And what is that? Ruth herself describes it below in her report to Naomi: for he said to me, "Do not come to your mother-in-law empty-handed." At the moment that is most crucial and dangerous to his very honor and position as the nation's leader, he is concerned about the bereaved widow who has been left alone, making sure that her daughter-in-law not return to her empty-handed!

The Midrash (*Ruth Rabbah* 7:4) comments on the meaning of the word ריקם (empty-handed): It is not to be compared to ריקם stated in connection with the Egyptians ("When you leave, you will not leave empty-handed" [*Shemos* 3:21]), nor to that stated regarding the Ivri servant ("You must not send him out empty-handed" [*Devarim* 15:13]), but rather to that of festival pilgrims ("And [the people] shall not [then] appear before Me empty-handed" [*Shemos* 23:15]). That is to say, with respect to those who left Egypt and the Ivri servant, it refers to great wealth and gifts, respectively. In regard to the pilgrims, however, the Torah requires only a symbolic amount. Similarly with Bo'az, who wanted to cheer up the bereaved widow and to show her that he had not forgotten her, even if only by sending a token of six barley grains. To him this was as important as appearing before God at the time of the pilgrimage festival!

In this small act, described in such plain and humble language, our Sages observed the height of greatness. They stated: As a reward for, "He measured out six barley grains and placed [them] upon her," he merited that there should descend from her six righteous men (*Ruth Rabbah* 7:2), one of them being Mashiach! A similar statement is paraphrased in the Targum (ibid.).

Herein lies a lesson about how to analyze the deeds of great people. Only our Sages knew how to judge the worth of actions that appear to be very insignificant, but that reveal all man's spiritual resources. What's more, the smaller the deeds, the more they reveal about one's purity of soul and nobleness, as discussed in the previous chapter. Such was Bo'az's deed that, while on the verge of ruin, he turned his attention to measuring out six barley grains into Ruth's kerchief, in order to bring some joy to Naomi.

That small act heralds redemption to the world. From the days of Kayin until the days of the Mashiach the world has been turning around one axis, the axis of extreme selfishness. People see each other as usurpers, as Kayin who killed Hevel, thinking that Hevel was encroaching upon his territory. The redemption of humankind will come through an opposite world view. Everyone will believe that his fellow is expanding the world for him, and that the good of his colleague always takes precedence over his own good. Great people will educate the masses to this Messianic philosophy. These great personages, right up to the greatest of them, Melech Ha-Mashiach, will all descend from Ruth and Bo'az, in whom this light glowed in all its splendor. As Chazal said: "Bo'az did his share, and Ruth did hers...so the Holy One, blessed is He, said, 'I must do Mine as well' " (*Ruth Rabbah* 7:7).

One more illustration will complete the picture. Our Sages point out that instead of "She...went to the city," it is written, "He...went to the city." They explain: "This teaches that he accompanied her, lest one of the lads accost her" (*Ruth Rabbah* 7:3). Until the very end, Bo'az continues forsaking his own honor to protect that of Ruth.

(טז) וַתָּבוֹא אֶל־חֲמוֹתָהּ וַתֹּאמֶר מִי־אַתְּ בִּתִּי וַתַּגֶּד־לָהּ אֵת
כָּל־אֲשֶׁר עָשָׂה־לָהּ הָאִישׁ: (יז) וַתֹּאמֶר שֵׁשׁ־הַשְּׂעֹרִים הָאֵלֶּה נָתַן
לִי כִּי אָמַר (אֵלַי קרי ולא כתיב) אַל־תָּבוֹאִי רֵיקָם אֶל־חֲמוֹתֵךְ:
(יח) וַתֹּאמֶר שְׁבִי בִתִּי עַד אֲשֶׁר תֵּדְעִין אֵיךְ יִפֹּל דָּבָר כִּי לֹא יִשְׁקֹט
הָאִישׁ כִּי־אִם־כִּלָּה הַדָּבָר הַיּוֹם:

(16) *[Ruth] came to her mother-in-law, and [her mother-in-law] asked [her], "Who are you, my daughter?" [Ruth] told her everything that the man had done for her.* (17) *She then said, "He gave me these six bar3ley grains, for he said [to me], 'Do not come to your mother-in-law empty-handed.' "* (18) *[Naomi] then said [to her], "Stay [here], my daughter, until you find out how the matter evolves, for the man will not rest until he has completed the matter today."*

16.-17. [Ruth] came to her mother-in-law, and [her mother-in-law] asked [her], "Who are you, my daughter?"

Naomi's sleep surely eluded her all that night. She lay down but her heart was awake, visions and fantasies passing before her eyes as she impatiently awaited Ruth's return. Her first question is: "Who are you, my daughter?" Whose are you — are you still mine, or do you belong to Bo'az? We may learn about Ruth's state of mind, while she was telling Naomi the consequences of her suggestion, from Naomi's closing words:

18. [Naomi] then said [to her], "Stay [here], my daughter, until you find out how the matter evolves...

According to the commentators, Naomi wants to pacify Ruth and prevent her from taking further action. Ruth apparently came back disappointed, because her explicit request, "spread your cloak over your maidservant [in marriage]," was not fulfilled, since Bo'az postponed the decision, resolving instead to involve an additional person in it, a redeemer who is closer than himself. Not so Naomi, who at the outset said only, "and he will tell you what you shall do," and this wish of hers was fulfilled. Bo'az had made his statement, and one may fully trust that he would faithfully live up to his words, for "The yes of the righteous is yes, and their no is no." Moreover, she is confident and certain "that the man will not rest until he has completed the matter today, without delays and postponements. As Chazal noted elsewhere, "The righteous perform all their deeds expeditiously" (*Bamidbar Rabbah* 10:17).

The Targum interprets our verse as follows: "Stay home with me, my daughter, until you find out what Heaven will decree and how the matter evolves, for the man will not rest until he has completed the matter for good today." From the additional words "for good," it appears that the Targum interprets the expression "כי אם כלה" ("until he has completed") as implying (as "ויכולו" does in the verses describing Creation) a concluded and perfect act. To Naomi it is as though her promise, "I [will] seek a place of contentment for you," had already been fulfilled, so confident was she of a favorable outcome, similar to (God's promise), "...will bless you with everything that you do" (*Devarim* 15:18). One must know, however, how much to "do" on one's own. It may have been appropriate to take a risky step, but that must suffice, for the matter is now in God's hand. Naomi is here referring not only to Bo'az, but mainly to Divine Providence. In other words, we have done our share and have transferred our efforts to the Creator, Who knows how to wrap up things. Let us therefore wait with confidence and trust, for time will elucidate and reveal to us "how the matter evolves," how things will unfold and yield the desired result through the good agent Bo'az.

ד (א) וּבֹעַז עָלָה הַשַּׁעַר וַיֵּשֶׁב שָׁם וְהִנֵּה הַגֹּאֵל עֹבֵר אֲשֶׁר דִּבֶּר־בֹּעַז וַיֹּאמֶר סוּרָה שְׁבָה־פֹּה פְּלֹנִי אַלְמֹנִי וַיָּסַר וַיֵּשֵׁב: (ב) וַיִּקַּח עֲשָׂרָה אֲנָשִׁים מִזִּקְנֵי הָעִיר וַיֹּאמֶר שְׁבוּ־פֹה וַיֵּשֵׁבוּ:

4 (1) *Bo'az, [meanwhile,] went up the gateway [of the court] and sat down there, and just then, the redeemer whom Bo'az had* *spoken of was passing by. [Bo'az] said [to him], "Mr. So-and-so! Come over [and] sit here," so he came over and sat down.* (2) *[Bo'az] then took ten of the elders of the city and said [to them], "Sit here," and they sat down.*

1. Bo'az, [meanwhile,] went up the gateway [of the court]...

Already at the beginning of this chapter we see how right Naomi was to say, "for the man will not rest until he has completed the matter today." Bo'az, whose remarkable deliberateness we have just observed, is now light as an eagle to do his duty. As soon as he and Ruth left the field, "when no one could yet recognize his fellowman," he went up the gateway, because "the zealous are early [to perform] mitzvos" (Pesachim 4a).

His great-grandson David had the same policy, as he swore and vowed "not to give sleep to his eyes" until he found a place for God — that is, where to build the Beis Ha-Mikdash (*Tehillim* 132:2–3). God had to appear to Nasan the Prophet one night and instruct him to go to David and prevent him from building a House of God (*Shemuel II* 7:5). As our Sages said: "The Holy One, blessed is He, said to Nasan, 'This man to whom I am sending you acts quickly. Go and tell him that he will not be the one to build the House, before he hires builders' " (*Yalkut Shimoni Shemuel* 143). Had Nasan not come to him that night, David would have jumped the gun and hired workers.

David inherited this enthusiasm for performing mitzvos from his ancestor Bo'az. Observe the value of zealousness: According to rabbinic tradition, Bo'az died that very night (*Yalkut Shimoni Ruth* 608). Had he not rushed to conclude the matter that day, he would never have married Ruth, similar to Chazal's statement: "Do not say, 'When I have leisure I shall study,' for you may never have leisure" (*Avos* 2:5).

Bo'az went up — Bo'az could probably have appointed an agent, since it was surely beneath his dignity to personally go to the court. The responsibility he had taken upon himself, however, outweighed his personal honor. For who knows the damage the agent might cause, by slightly altering his sender's words, or due to the redeemer's embarrassment in front of a stranger. This may even be inferred from Bo'az's very words to the redeemer: "Now I said [to myself that] I shall make you aware" — "I and not an agent" (*Midrash Lekach Tov*), because relatives can talk the essentials over frankly. One who performs a task himself hastens it toward its conclusion; sending an agent, however, is a way of ridding oneself of it. In addition to all these misgivings, the fact is that "it is more meritorious to perform a mitzvah by oneself than through one's agent" (*Kiddushin* 41a), due to one's fondness for the mitzvah. As we learned concerning Avraham, "And he saddled his donkey" (*Bereshis* 22:3): Although he had many servants, he saddled it himself, because he was going to fulfill God's command (see *Midrash Rabbah* there). So, too, did Bo'az act when he was going to perform a deed of kindness: He did not worry about lowering the court's dignity or about "what people would say." That is why Scripture stresses that "Bo'az went up" — he, personally.

And just then [והנה — lit. behold], the redeemer whom Bo'az had spoken of was passing by — The word והנה, as explained above (2:4), introduces a novelty: Suddenly, the redeemer appears. As our Sages wondered: "Was he really standing behind the gate?...Had he been even at the end of the world, the Holy One, blessed is He, would have flown him and brought him, so that that righteous man [Bo'az] should not sit there in sorrow" (*Ruth Rabbah* 7:7). In another source, Chazal are quoted as having said: "God immediately dispatched an angel, who brought Tov" (*Midrash Lekach Tov*). An "incident," in the sense of an angel, was caused by Divine Providence. Scripture also hints that Bo'az's speech was the basis for what happened. He had said to Ruth, "והיה בבקר — and [it will happen] in the morning" (3:13), and indeed, the next morning, "[behold,] the redeemer whom Bo'az had spoken of was passing by." In other words, his words induced the redeemer's appearance at that particular time. And thus was Naomi's trust in Divine Providence confirmed as well.

2. [Bo'az] then took ten of the elders of the city...

Our Sages comment that Bo'az gathered the elders to clarify before them the law of " 'a male Ammoni,' to exclude a female; 'a male Mo'avi,' to exclude a female." A quorum of ten was required for the marriage blessings. This is another indication of Bo'az's zealousness: He sees to it that everything should be completely ready for the marriage ceremony, even before knowing for whom — for the redeemer, or for himself!

(ג) וַיֹּאמֶר לַגֹּאֵל חֶלְקַת הַשָּׂדֶה אֲשֶׁר לְאָחִינוּ לֶאֱלִימֶלֶךְ מָכְרָה
נָעֳמִי הַשָּׁבָה מִשְּׂדֵה מוֹאָב: (ד) וַאֲנִי אָמַרְתִּי אֶגְלֶה אָזְנְךָ לֵאמֹר
קְנֵה נֶגֶד הַיֹּשְׁבִים וְנֶגֶד זִקְנֵי עַמִּי אִם־תִּגְאַל גְּאָל וְאִם־לֹא יִגְאַל
הַגִּידָה לִּי וְאֵדְעָ כִּי אֵין זוּלָתְךָ לִגְאוֹל וְאָנֹכִי אַחֲרֶיךָ וַיֹּאמֶר אָנֹכִי
אֶגְאָל: (ה) וַיֹּאמֶר בֹּעַז בְּיוֹם־קְנוֹתְךָ הַשָּׂדֶה מִיַּד נָעֳמִי וּמֵאֵת רוּת
הַמּוֹאֲבִיָּה אֵשֶׁת־הַמֵּת קָנִיתִי (קָנִיתָ ק') לְהָקִים שֵׁם־הַמֵּת עַל־
נַחֲלָתוֹ: (ו) וַיֹּאמֶר הַגֹּאֵל לֹא אוּכַל לִגְאוֹל־(יתיר ו') לִי פֶּן־אַשְׁחִית
אֶת־נַחֲלָתִי גְּאַל־לְךָ אַתָּה אֶת־גְּאֻלָּתִי כִּי לֹא־אוּכַל לִגְאֹל:

(3) *He then said to the redeemer, "The section of the field that belonged to our brother, Elimelech — Naomi, who returned from the field of Mo'av, has offered [it] for sale.* (4) *Now, I said [to myself that] I shall make you aware as follows: Make an act of acquisition in front of those seated [here] and in front of the elders of my people. If you [are willing to] redeem, [then] redeem, but if [you] are not [willing to] redeem, tell me [now so that] I may know, for there is no one [closer] than you to act as redeemer, and I am after you." He replied, "I shall redeem."* (5) *Bo'az then said, "On the day you acquire the field from Naomi, you [will also need to] acquire [it] from Ruth the Mo'aviyah [and to marry her], so as to perpetuate the name of the deceased on his inherited property."* (6) *The redeemer replied, "I cannot redeem [the field] for myself, so that I do not ruin [the name of] my descendants. You redeem for yourself what I was to redeem, for I cannot redeem."*

3.–6. He then said to the redeemer, "The section of the field

that belonged to our brother, Elimelech," etc. The redeemer
replied, "I cannot redeem..."

From the way Bo'az negotiates, we are again able to detect
his righteousness and purity of soul, as well as how he
eliminates his self-interest for the benefit of others. It has
already been pointed out in the previous chapter that Bo'az
had wanted to redeem Ruth, but that the closer relative had
priority. Accordingly, Bo'az should have influenced things to
where the redeemer would refuse. However, he is acting to
the contrary, and actually trying to convince the redeemer to
agree! As someone who is an expert in psychology and
persuasion, he does not immediately propose everything, but
mentions only the field, something which the redeemer
would find it easy to redeem. After the latter agrees to do so,
Bo'az goes from the easy to the difficult, explaining what is
involved — that is, that along with purchasing the field, he
would have to perpetuate the name of the deceased on his
inherited property. Only after hearing the redeemer's refusal,
"I cannot redeem," along with the plea, "You redeem for
yourself what I was to redeem," does Bo'az accept the
responsibility contentedly.

So that I do not ruin [the name of] my descendants — The
redeemer has an explicit excuse for refusing: "So that I do not
ruin [the name of] my descendants." As Chazal explain: "The
former ones died only because they married them. Should I
then marry her? God forbid; I will not contaminate my
children" (*Ruth Rabbah* 7:10). He had not adequately
assimilated the new law, and was still worried that this would
taint his offspring.

His misunderstanding was not accidental. Deep down
inside, he did not wish to redeem. That is why he did not
fully investigate the law permitting the female proselyte and
used the excuse that it would taint his descendants. His inner
resistance was covered by an imaginary cloak of Torah. Our
Sages explained: "[He was called] אלמוני [So-and-so] because
he was אלם [ignorant, lit. 'dumb'] of the words of the Torah"
(*Ruth Rabbah* 7:7). Torah truth did not come out of his mouth.

Due to his ignorance in God's Torah, he lost all benefits — the kingdom of the House of David and the inheritance of the Mashiach.

Even in our Scriptures he is left with the vague title, "Peloni Almoni [Mr. So-and-so]," as explained here by Rashi: "His name is not mentioned, because he refused to redeem." Several commentators did not understand what Rashi meant, and asked: Were there not others who did evil but had their names mentioned anyway? The answer is that their name was indeed mentioned, for everlasting ignominy, whereas Peloni Almoni, who had the opportunity to perform an act of kindness, but did not do so, did not even merit being honored with the immortalization of his name. He remains unknown, disappearing into oblivion, while Scripture immortalizes Bo'az with fame and renown.

(ז) וְזֹאת לְפָנִים בְּיִשְׂרָאֵל עַל־הַגְּאוּלָּה וְעַל־הַתְּמוּרָה לְקַיֵּם כָּל־דָּבָר שָׁלַף אִישׁ נַעֲלוֹ וְנָתַן לְרֵעֵהוּ וְזֹאת הַתְּעוּדָה בְּיִשְׂרָאֵל: (ח) וַיֹּאמֶר הַגֹּאֵל לְבֹעַז קְנֵה־לָךְ וַיִּשְׁלֹף נַעֲלוֹ: (ט) וַיֹּאמֶר בֹּעַז לַזְּקֵנִים וְכָל־הָעָם עֵדִים אַתֶּם הַיּוֹם כִּי קָנִיתִי אֶת־כָּל־אֲשֶׁר לֶאֱלִימֶלֶךְ וְאֵת כָּל־אֲשֶׁר לְכִלְיוֹן וּמַחְלוֹן מִיַּד נָעֳמִי: (י) וְגַם אֶת־רוּת הַמֹּאֲבִיָּה אֵשֶׁת מַחְלוֹן קָנִיתִי לִי לְאִשָּׁה לְהָקִים שֵׁם־הַמֵּת עַל־נַחֲלָתוֹ וְלֹא־יִכָּרֵת שֵׁם־הַמֵּת מֵעִם אֶחָיו וּמִשַּׁעַר מְקוֹמוֹ עֵדִים אַתֶּם הַיּוֹם:

(7) *And this [procedure] was the time-honored practice among Yisrael regarding sales and exchanges, to validate any [transaction]: One man would remove his shoe and give it to his fellowman; and this was the method of testification [of a transaction] among Yisrael.* (8) *The redeemer then said to Bo'az, "Make an act of acquisition for yourself," and [so] he removed his shoe.* (9) *Bo'az then said to the elders and all the people [present], "You are witnesses today that I have acquired from Naomi everything that belonged to Elimelech, and everything that belonged to Kilyon and Machlon.* (10) *And I have also*

acquired for myself Ruth the Mo'aviyah, the wife of Machlon, as a wife, to perpetuate the name of the deceased on his inherited property, so that the name of the deceased not be obliterated from among his brethren and from the gateway of his local [court]; you are witnesses today."

9. Bo'az then said to the elders and all the people [present], "You are witnesses today..."

Here we see Bo'az in a new light, as a skillful man of action who handles his affairs cleverly and with prudence. He gives great publicity to his acquisition and redemption, asking for the approval of the elders and all the people, to prevent any protests or complaints.

Speaking first about acquiring the field, he details: "I have acquired from Naomi everything that belonged to Elimelech, and everything that belonged to Kilyon and Machlon." Chazal explain his choice of words: "Why did he mention Kilyon first? This conveys that one must beware of evil members of the family; it was to prevent Orpah from claiming that the field belonged to her husband, or her son from claiming to be Kilyon's son" (*Ruth Zuta*). Bo'az clarifies his purchase very precisely, mentioning Kilyon first, because of the greater apprehension connected to that part of the deal.

Since the righteous are very careful not to appropriate others' property, they take pains to specify very precisely what is theirs, because it is very easy to enter into complications and become entangled in a mess. Clarifying everything perfectly is one of the Torah's foundations, so that there will be no room for protest after one's actions. Similarly, our Sages pointed out in Avraham's dealings with Efron the Chitti: "Look at how much ink and how many quills it took to write 'the Children of Ches' ten times! This comes to teach that clarifying the purchase of a righteous person is akin to fulfilling the Ten Commandments" (*Bereshis Rabbah* 58). Generally speaking, every illustration and expression of the prophets enlightens us in Torah outlook and practice.

Bo'az needed the approval of the elders and the people

concerning the redemption of Ruth more than in the acquisition of the field, for it appeared odd that the old judge would marry the Mo'aviyah girl. There was reason to worry about people speaking unfavorably of him, and finding fault with him, as indeed did Almoni. That is why Bo'az explains publicly that he has come only to fulfill the mitzvah of the Torah to perpetuate the name of the deceased. Of course, this was also a way to properly publicize the novel halachah.

We may see how essential this was from the fact that a few generations later, Do'eg the Edomi would still cast aspersions on David's lineage (*see Yevamos* 76b). Now who is able to say what might have happened had Bo'az married Ruth without the consent of all the people!

(יא) וַיֹּאמְרוּ כָּל־הָעָם אֲשֶׁר־בַּשַּׁעַר וְהַזְּקֵנִים עֵדִים יִתֵּן יְהֹוָה
אֶת־הָאִשָּׁה הַבָּאָה אֶל־בֵּיתֶךָ כְּרָחֵל ׀ וּכְלֵאָה אֲשֶׁר בָּנוּ שְׁתֵּיהֶם
אֶת־בֵּית יִשְׂרָאֵל וַעֲשֵׂה־חַיִל בְּאֶפְרָתָה וּקְרָא־שֵׁם בְּבֵית לָחֶם:

(11) *All the people who were at the gateway [of the court] and the elders — the witnesses — then said, "May the Eternal grant [that] the woman who is entering your home [be] like Rachel and Leah, who both created the House of Yisrael; and become prosperous in Efras and famous in Beis Lechem."*

11. All the people who were at the gateway [of the court] and the elders — the witnesses — then said...

One can feel the joy and excitement that accompany the joint approval of the people and the elders. Their response seemingly serves also as a consolation to Bo'az, as if they are saying to him: We are witnesses before God and all future generations that this deed is as lofty as those involving Ya'akov and Rachel, and Yehudah and Tamar, respectively, which also seemed peculiar and open to criticism. We therefore wish upon you similar consequences, for one of those relationships built the House of Yisrael, while out of the other sprouted forth the tribe of Yehudah, to whom royalty has been promised.

May the Eternal grant [that] the woman who is entering your home [be] like Rachel and Leah, who both created the House of Yisrael — Just as the lineage of Rachel and Leah played no role in their building of the Jewish nation — though their father was Lavan the Arami, "who had wished to uproot everything" — so too shall be Ruth, despite her being from a nation with whom intermarriage is forbidden. Here we are reminded of the response of Bo'az, as brought by Chazal, when Ruth said to him, "though I am not even [as worthy] as one of your maidservants": "God forbid! You are not [as one] of the maidservants [אמהות], but [as one] of the matriarchs [אימהות]" (see above, 2:13, 14). Here his words came true: The people perceived that Ruth was like Rachel and Leah, in that she would raise anew the people of Yisrael. Actually, the House of Yisrael was already built and standing, so what else did they want? It was rather a sign that they anticipated someone who would mend the breaches in that House, making it like a new building. In truth, this couple was privileged to become the progenitors of David, who has been set beside Avraham, Yitzchak, and Ya'akov.

(יב) וִיהִי בֵיתְךָ כְּבֵית פֶּרֶץ אֲשֶׁר־יָלְדָה תָמָר לִיהוּדָה מִן־הַזֶּרַע אֲשֶׁר יִתֵּן יְהוָה לְךָ מִן־הַנַּעֲרָה הַזֹּאת:

(12) *"And may your household be like the House of Peretz, whom Tamar bore to Yehudah, from the children that the Eternal will give to you from this young woman."*

12. And may your household be like the House of Peretz, whom Tamar bore to Yehudah...

This is like what happened with Yehudah who had taken Tamar — that select woman, whom Divine Providence wanted to be the mother of the royal family of Yisrael — for his son. His sons, however, interfered with God's secret plan through their misdeeds. Yet we see how Providence spins its plot, to the extent that all man's deeds are for naught, whereas God's prevail: Tamar again wound up in Yehudah's portion. So did Providence arrange things in a remarkable way to draw Ruth into the bosom of Yisrael.

In what the people and the elders emphasize in their blessing — "like the House of Peretz whom Tamar bore to Yehudah" — there is a hint of the comparison between Tamar and Ruth. Both had risked their honor and name, trying in similar fashion to attach themselves to the tribe of Yehudah and this particular family. In the words of our Sages: "Two women dedicated themselves to the tribe of Yehudah — Tamar and Ruth" (*Yalkut* to *Ruth* 411). Ruth was therefore worthy of continuing the House of Peretz whom Tamar bore. Thus, it is evident that the people and the elders hung both crowns on this union of Ruth and Bo'az: the crown of the Jewish people and that of the Kingdom of Yisrael.

"LIKE RACHEL AND LEAH, WHO BOTH CREATED THE HOUSE OF YISRAEL"

With these remarkable words, the prophet who wrote the Megillah opened for us a little window in the wall of the distant past, one through which we may peek into the inner world of the Jewish people of those ancient days.

It was the first time that a proselyte had come from an repressive and hostile nation, the relationship with which was worse than that of all other surrounding nations. Furthermore, the Torah explicitly forbids marriage with their proselytes, a fact that strengthened the dividing wall between the two nations. And it is brought in Chazal that following the destruction of the Beis Ha-Mikdash the Mo'avim took revenge upon the Torah because of that law. There was also a protest among the Jewish people against Ruth the Mo'aviyah, even in the time of David. Ruth herself could not imagine that Bo'az would pay attention to her, as she expressed her surprise: "Why do you regard me favorably by taking notice of me, when I am a foreigner?" Naomi, too, doubted such a possibility, compelling her to make what was certainly an extremely unconventional suggestion.

Yet, we find that the people and the elders reacted in a most unexpected way. They put the Mo'aviyah proselyte on the same level as our matriarchs Rachel and Leah, as well as the illustrious Tamar, who had become so established in the tribe of Yehudah, even to the extent that all its princes descended from her. What is more, these words are said after Ruth had come at night to Bo'az's barn, an act that appeared to be immoral. We even note that she herself was deathly worried about the people's wrath, Bo'az having had to comfort her with, "Do not be afraid." Yet the people did not merely withhold their indignation; they even honored and venerated her beyond description. And what for? The Megillah offers no reason, except the words of Bo'az: "for all [the elders of] my people [who sit at] the gateway [of the court] are aware that you are a woman of fortitude." The people perceived in her their ideal, "a woman of fortitude," with all that wonderful appellation implies. That served as a sufficient reason to waive the settling of all accounts between Yisrael and Mo'av, and to adorn this proselyte with splendor.

This is reiterated in the blessing they gave Bo'az, "from the children that the Eternal will give to you from this young woman." Chazal explain: They said: "May all the children that the Holy One, blessed is He, gives you, be from this righteous woman" (Ruth Rabbah 7:14). This shows how much respect Yisrael had for Ruth's moral values. It also highlights the Jewish people's ability to rise above all other considerations and to discern the merits of true virtues.

Our Sages noticed additional allusions in these passages to the great importance of a virtuous woman: "May the Eternal grant [that] the woman" — Rav Acha said: "Whoever marries an upright woman is as if he has kept the entire Torah, from beginning to end. It is to him that the following verse (Tehillim 128) applies: 'Your wife shall be as a fruitful vine....' " That is why the verses of the chapter entitled, "A Woman of Valor" (Mishlei 31), is arranged alphabetically, containing every letter from Aleph to Tav. Additionally, each generation may be redeemed only in the merit of its righteous women, as it is stated, "He has recalled His kindness and His faithfulness to the House of Yisrael" (*Tehillim* 98:3); it does not say "to the Children of Yisrael," but "to the House of Yisrael" (*Yalkut Shimoni* 606). This statement of our Sages may be explained as follows: From the fact that the prophet emphasized, "like Rachel and Leah, who both created the House of Yisrael," Chazal sensed that marrying a virtuous woman is a guarantee for the fulfillment of the entire Torah, on which the House of Yisrael is built. Similarly, when the Torah was given, God's first appeal to Moshe was, "So shall you say to the House of Ya'akov" (*Shemos* 19:3), meaning, say Chazal, "to the women" (Mechilta, there) As was noted, the chapter "A Woman of Valor" contains the entire alphabet, to indicate that the observance of the whole Torah depends on her. And since the above-mentioned verse in Tehillim connects the Redemption to God's recalling kindness to the House of Yisrael, which is built by virtuous women, it follows that they are the ones who bring the Redemption. This proclamation by our Sages is an ode of praise to the upright woman, much as the chapter "A Woman of Valor" in the Book of Mishlei.

(יג) וַיִּקַּח בֹּעַז אֶת־רוּת וַתְּהִי־לוֹ לְאִשָּׁה וַיָּבֹא אֵלֶיהָ וַיִּתֵּן יְהֹוָה לָהּ הֵרָיוֹן וַתֵּלֶד בֵּן:

(13) *Bo'az then took Ruth, and she became his wife. He married her, and the Eternal caused her to become pregnant, and she gave birth to a son.*

13. Bo'az then took Ruth...

According to Chazal, the prophet is underscoring the suitability of this union: Bo'az then took Ruth — she was designated for him; and she became his wife — she was appropriate for him (*Midrash Lekach Tov*). The Eternal caused her to become pregnant, and she gave birth to a son — God's name is mentioned in connection with this pregnancy. It was with special Divine Providence that a son was born from this union, for according to a tradition of Chazal, Ruth had been barren (*Ruth Rabbah* 7:14).

The Midrash states: Rabbi Berechiah said: "This is what the two great men, Rabbi Eliezer and Rabbi Yehoshua expounded. Rabbi Eliezer said, 'Bo'az did his share, Ruth did her share, and Naomi did her share, so The Holy One, blessed is He, said, I must do Mine as well' " (*Ruth Rabbah* 7:7). Thus did our Sages summarize the actions of the three heroes, who are extolled by the Megillah, confirming that the prophet had established that the actions of each of them totally conformed with God's will. That is to say, all three had attained, through their deeds, the greatest level of altruism that could be expected of them. In addition, each had complemented the other's merits — as opposed to the three "fallen heroes" (Chazal) mentioned in the beginning of the Megillah, Elimelech and his two sons, all three of whom blundered and caused each other to falter as well.

How did Naomi "do her share"? Her very name [נעמי] sings her praises, for "her deeds were fair and pleasant [נעימים]." Through her pleasant deeds she caused Ruth to leave behind all that had been dear and beloved to her and to cling to Naomi instead. These deeds are not spelled out in the Megillah. Let us examine her actions that are revealed in the Megillah. Following the decline of the entire family it was difficult to expect her to return to Beis Lechem where she would become a cause for everyone to shake their heads: "Is this Naomi?" And to have to resort to gifts of the poor, whereas she had had an honored position in Mo'av, as seen from the words, "She left the place," which imply that (as with Ya'akov; see Rashi to *Bereshis* 28:10) when she left, the city's glory and majesty departed. Ostensibly, due to her aristocratic daughters-in-law, she could have lived there very well. Besides, we find that Elimelech's death and her sons' marriages to gentile women did not cause her to return to her country, as she probably had resigned herself to living in Mo'av, due to a misguided personal philosophy. Coming back following the death of her sons was much more pitiful, as we detect in her confession: "Do not call me Naomi (pleasantness)! Call me Marah (bitterness)... I left full [of possessions], and the Eternal brought me back empty-handed." There was therefore a real chance that Naomi would be destroyed as were the rest of her family, forever erasing all of them from the lineage of the House of Yisrael. It did not happen, however; rather, "[Naomi] arose," thus reviving not only herself, by having the son (born to Ruth) accredited to her name — "A son was born to Naomi" (4:17) — but the entire family, for in the end even their going to Mo'av was inscribed for the good (see above on 1:1, "A man...went"). It was worth it for them to jump into the sea in order to find the pearl called Ruth. Ruth was drawn to the Jewish people by Naomi who, after the death of her sons, was able to turn her daughter-in-law into a daughter for herself. This serves as a model of human relations in the world, as it will be in the long-awaited era of the Redemption. Naomi, who appeared in the Megillah as a second Iyov, emerged from the crucible of afflictions graciously and honorably: "Naomi did her share."

"Ruth did her share" — She eschewed her past and her future and clung to Naomi; she renounced her lineage and went to the field to glean among the poor; she forsook her womanly honor and went to Bo'az's barn on the advice of Naomi. All this showed her innocence, righteousness, and humbleness. She does not set her sights on high goals, as stated also by her descendant David: "O Eternal, my heart was not haughty, nor my eyes lofty" (*Tehillim* 131:1). Neither does she expect reward for her deeds. She is always ready to sacrifice all she has in order to perform an act of kindness, as is evident from everything she does. This is actually the Messianic goal, that one rise above his egocentrism. In the Megillah itself, both Naomi and Bo'az express the fact that Ruth was a living example of the ideal person (see end of chap. 1, and chap. 2).

"Bo'az did his share" — Bo'az, too, embodied love of man and honoring him. We saw how he treated the Mo'aviyah girl who gleaned in his field: how he welcomed her in word and deed, blessed (instead of cursed) her in the barn, and how he patiently measured out barley for Naomi, "for he said, 'Do not come to your mother-in-law empty-handed.' " This despite the fact that every slight delay could have brought him shame and disgrace. We also observed how enthusiastic, industrious, and scrupulous he was in carrying out the kind deed and everything else explained above. Though all his efforts, from beginning to end, seem trivial to us, Chazal, with their discerning eye, considered them to be paragons of man's ability to control himself, his weaknesses and inclinations, to benefit others. Thus, Bo'az, too, prevailed when put to the supreme test, receiving the Divinely inspired seal of approval: "Bo'az did his share."

All these three heroes performed their missions within a small family circle, but "the Holy One, blessed is He, did His share" as well: He wove an eternal web, creating the Messianic chain of the House of David. The Hand of Providence used their very deeds to tie one thread to another, to turn the wheels in the desired direction, and to culminate the whole chain of events in a miraculous pregnancy.

(יד) וַתֹּאמַרְנָה הַנָּשִׁים אֶל־נָעֳמִי בָּרוּךְ יְהֹוָה אֲשֶׁר לֹא הִשְׁבִּית לָךְ גֹּאֵל הַיּוֹם וְיִקָּרֵא שְׁמוֹ בְּיִשְׂרָאֵל: (טו) וְהָיָה לָךְ לְמֵשִׁיב נֶפֶשׁ וּלְכַלְכֵּל אֶת־שֵׂיבָתֵךְ כִּי כַלָּתֵךְ אֲשֶׁר־אֲהֵבַתֶךְ יְלָדַתּוּ אֲשֶׁר־הִיא טוֹבָה לָךְ מִשִּׁבְעָה בָּנִים: (טז) וַתִּקַּח נָעֳמִי אֶת־הַיֶּלֶד וַתְּשִׁתֵהוּ בְחֵיקָהּ וַתְּהִי־לוֹ לְאֹמֶנֶת:

(14) *The women then said to Naomi, "The Eternal [has shown Himself to be] the Source of blessing, that He has not deprived you today of a redeemer, and may [this child] become famous among Yisrael.* (15) *And may he be for you [like] a living re-embodiment [of Machlon], and provide [for you in] your old age, for your daughter-in-law who loves you gave birth to him, [and] she is better to you than [even] seven sons."* (16) *Naomi then took the child and placed him in her bosom, and she became his nurse.*

14. The women then said to Naomi, "The Eternal [has shown Himself to be] the Source of blessing, that He has not deprived you today of a redeemer..."

This is not merely the blessing of chattering women, but a voice from the depths of the people: "The talk of women is the talk of the people." The people realized and blessed, and the prophet confirmed it. That is why Chazal construe it as prophecy: "Just as this day dominates in the heavens, so shall your progeny dominate and rule over Israel forever" (*Ruth Rabbah* 7:15). The women are prophesying that from this wondrous conception the redeemer will sprout and arise, he whose rule in the world will be like that of the day by the light of the sun. The latter spreads its rule over the heavens and vanquishes the darkness of the night, as it is written, "the sun in all its strength" (*Shofetim* 5:31). So will the light of truth and kindness cut through all darkness and redeem the world. On what did the women base such a lofty prophecy as applying to the son born that day to Bo'az and Ruth? They saw and recognized that such a phenomenon, accompanied by so many great acts of kindness, must produce the root of the Mashiach.

The women's blessing, therefore, complements the preceding blessing of the people and the elders, praising Ruth with the acclamation of redemption as well. Here we may glimpse the inner character of the Jewish people. We see how an entire nation, adults as well as children, bestow the highest of praises on a daughter of a despised and hated nation, in the merit of her moral qualities. They will not be blinded by any racist or political considerations. This is the appraisement of a holy nation rising above the plane of mundane living. Had the Megillah been written only to reveal to us the spirit of the people of Yisrael of that era, it would have sufficed!

Such is the profundity of Chazal's statement: "Rabbi Huna said: It was due to the women's blessings that David's lineage was not severed entirely in the days of Asalyah" (*Ruth Rabbah* 7:15). Apparently, in those days many people greatly resented the royal House of David, enabling Asalyah to annihilate almost the whole royal family (*Melachim II* 11:1–3). Through Divine inspiration Chazal discerned that Asalyah's failure was due to the women's blessing of the distant past, in the days of Ruth. That blessing instilled in the people the realization that, despite all criticism and accusations that might be made against the Davidic dynasty, in the end it alone bears the foundation for the Redemption of Yisrael and the world.

(יז) וַתִּקְרֶאנָה לוֹ הַשְּׁכֵנוֹת שֵׁם לֵאמֹר יֻלַּד־בֵּן לְנָעֳמִי וַתִּקְרֶאנָה שְׁמוֹ עוֹבֵד הוּא אֲבִי־יִשַׁי אֲבִי דָוִד:

(17) *The neighboring women gave him a name, saying, "A son was born to Naomi." They named him Oved; he is the father of Yishai, the father of David.*

17. The neighboring women gave him a name...

We have seen how much importance our Sages attributed to the women's blessing in the preceding verses. It goes without saying that the neighbors mentioned here are also not plain old women, but those who express the spirit of the Jewish people. Again, the prophet, author of the Megillah, validates their words.

Two things the women said were inscribed for posterity. First, that the boy that was born was ascribed to Naomi: "...saying, 'A son was born to Naomi.' " Since she had given the advice and was the cause of the union, it is considered as though she had borne the son. Similarly, it is stated concerning Moshe that the daughters of Yisro told their father, "A Mitzri (Egyptian) man saved us" (*Shemos* 2:19). Chazal explain: "Who caused this man to come to us? The Mitzri whom he killed" (*Shemos Rabbah* 1:39). One of the tenets of Judaism is that the point of departure must be determined, because it is the key factor in the cause and effect chain.

As did the previous blessings, this shout of the neighbors, too, expresses joy: "A son was born to Naomi," and this means that there remains a name and a remembrance to this illustrious family. This sheds light on the people's attitude toward Elimelech's family after it had left the country. Had their departure evoked only criticism and anger among Yisrael, the latter would not have looked favorably upon all that befell that family. The fact that everyone regarded the birth of a son to Naomi as a consolation proves that they had been sad and sorrowed by the departure of Elimelech and his family. That is why they all rejoiced upon seeing the new shoot. So now, after all these events, Naomi ceased being "Marah" (bitterness) and became "Naomi" (pleasantness) once again. Moreover, her current situation was even better than her former one, as the women said to her concerning Ruth: "She is better to you than [even] seven sons."

THEY NAMED HIM OVED

The second remarkable thing was the name the neighbors gave the baby: Oved. Our Sages explain the significance of that name: He was named for his father, who had been old, had married a woman for the sake of Heaven, and was called an Oved (servant) of God; and for his mother, as it is written, "You will once again see [the difference] between a righteous person and a wicked one, [and] between the one who serves God and the one who does not serve him" (*Malachi* 3:18) — that is, between Ruth and Orpah, for Orpah became a disgrace whereas Ruth attached herself to God. That is why he was named Oved. A righteous man married a righteous woman and bore a perfectly righteous son. His third [descendant] was chosen by the Holy One, blessed is He, as it is stated: "He chose David, His servant" (*Midrash Lekach Tov*).

The Gemara clarifies this Midrash: Bar Hei Hei said to Hillel, "What is meant by, 'You will once again see [the difference] between a righteous person and a wicked one, [and] between the one who serves God and the one who does not serve Him'? — 'A righteous person' is the same as 'one who serves God'; 'the wicked' is the same as 'one who does not serve Him'!" He answered him: " 'One who serves Him' and 'one who does not serve Him' both refer to people who are perfectly righteous; but he who repeats his learning a hundred times is not to be compared with him who repeats it a hundred and one times" (*Chagigah* 9b). This informs us that "Servant of God" implies the highest degree of perfection, and that one may be perfectly righteous, but if there is lacking even one iota in his efforts to attain his utmost in Torah and good deeds, he is not on the level of a "Servant of God," which is man's ultimate goal, as it is written regarding the Revelation at Mount Sinai: "You will [all] serve God on this mountain" (*Shemos* 3:12). Only a select few have been privileged to earn the title of "Servant of God." Some had given themselves that appellation, but Scripture did not endorse it (*Sifri Va'eschanan*).

Now we understand the words of the Prophet Malachi. In his days, some people remonstrated against the ways of Divine Providence: "You said, It is worthless serving God, and what monetary gain is there [for us] that we observed His restrictions..." (*Malachi* 3:14). The prophet answers them that a day will come when "You will once again see" — In the end the whole world will see the difference between the righteous and the wicked, and between one who serves God and one who does not, a difference which is sometimes very small. The Midrash uses Orpah and Ruth as an example. In the beginning both appeared to be equal in their dedication, and Naomi's appreciation of both — "May the Eternal grant you" — remains on the record in the Megillah. Orpah, however, did not pass the ultimate test, the one that defied logic, causing such a schism between them, to the point where one became the ancestress of David, and the other, of Golias. This is a cogent example of: "You will once again see [the difference] between...the one who serves God and the one who does not serve Him."

Yet, in the case of Bo'az and Ruth, the neighbors and the people determined, and the prophet who wrote the Megillah confirmed, that both were not only perfectly righteous, but

"Servants of God" as well. Man's ultimate goal served as a
guiding light for all their deeds, which they performed with
no ulterior motives whatsoever. (It has already been pointed
out that the word אלי [me] is missing in Ruth's response to
Naomi, "Whatever you tell [me] to do I shall do" [3:5],
meaning that she had no self-interest in the matter.) Their
union was completely devoid of human desires, so that the
baby born from it could not be defined in terms of "in sin did
my mother conceive me" (Tehillim 51:7). Hence, he was
named Oved, which is a reference to his father and mother,
as well as to his birth itself. Also his offshoot, Mashiach, son
of David, is prophetically referred to as "My Servant."
Scripture here adds, "He is the father of Yishai, the father of
David" — that is, both Yishai and David were already
included in his essence.

(יח) וְאֵלֶּה תּוֹלְדוֹת פָּרֶץ פֶּרֶץ הוֹלִיד אֶת־חֶצְרוֹן: (יט) וְחֶצְרוֹן הוֹלִיד
אֶת־רָם וְרָם הוֹלִיד אֶת־עַמִּינָדָב: (כ) וְעַמִּינָדָב הוֹלִיד אֶת־נַחְשׁוֹן
וְנַחְשׁוֹן הוֹלִיד אֶת־שַׂלְמָה: (כא) וְשַׂלְמוֹן הוֹלִיד אֶת־בֹּעַז וּבֹעַז
הוֹלִיד אֶת־עוֹבֵד: (כב) וְעֹבֵד הוֹלִיד אֶת־יִשַׁי וְיִשַׁי הוֹלִיד אֶת־דָּוִד:

(18) *And these are the descendants of Peretz: Peretz fathered
Chetzron;* (19) *and Chetzron fathered Ram, and Ram fathered
Amminadav;* (20) *and Amminadav fathered Nachshon, and
Nachshon fathered Salmah;* (21) *and Salmon fathered Bo'az, and
Bo'az fathered Oved;* (22) *and Oved fathered Yishai, and Yishai
fathered David.*

KING DAVID

"And these are the descendants of Peretz...
and Yishai fathered David."

Ten Generations

In listing the generations, the prophet begins a new era
with Peretz. Scripture enumerates ten generations from
Peretz to David, repeating each name, as if to grant each of

them a double eternal remembrance. Chazal stated: "Whoever's name is repeated has a share in this world and in the next world (*Bereshis Rabbah* 38:18). Among these ten generations of righteous men there are names that stand out forever due to their greatness and renown, such as Nachshon, son of Amminadav, whose sister the Torah credits Aharon with marrying. Nachshon was also the first of the leaders of the tribe of Yehudah, and he is renowned for what Chazal told us about his valor and self-sacrifice before the splitting of the Sea of Reeds. And who is greater than Bo'az, the ideal man, who was called "Servant of God"! Nevertheless, all the generations listed here are inferior to David, concerning whom our Sages said: This may be illustrated with a parable about a king who lost a priceless pearl. What did he do? He gathered the soil and sifted it in a sieve until he found the pearl. So said the Holy One, blessed is He, to David, "Why did I have to document the genealogy of Peretz, Chetzron, Ram, Amminadav, Nachshon, Salmon, Bo'az, Oved, and Yishai? Only because of you! — 'I have found David, My servant' " (end of *Ruth Rabbah*).

David was not just a random person who happened to be born with superior characteristics. A row of generations points in his direction, with God sifting and checking each of them, until finding the sought-after soul, shining gloriously like a pearl.

"WHERE DID I FIND HIM? — IN SEDOM"

The formation of David, King of Yisrael's soul, began long before, also by way of "finding." This is mentioned elsewhere by Chazal: "...and your two daughters who are [present; lit. 'found'] here [with you]" (*Bereshis* 19:15). Said Rav Tuvia bar Rabbi Yitzchak, "Two finds — Ruth the Mo'aviyah and Na'amah the Ammonis." Said Rabbi Yitzchak: "I have found David, My servant" (*Tehillim* 89:21). "Where did I find him? In Sedom" (*Bereshis Rabbah* 50:16).

How important and remarkable are these words of our

Sages! The Divine Inspiration declares, "I have found David, My servant," as if proclaiming the Great Proclamation: "I have found the purpose of the world!" Then our Sages come and tell us that this "find" was discovered among the refuse of human corruption, upon which Divine judgment rained down fire and brimstone, turning the entire area into an eternally cursed one. What is more, the "finding" of David is connected with the exploits of Lot's daughters. The Holy One, blessed is He, so to speak, sought appropriate human material from which to form the God of Ya'akov's Mashiach, and the Sweet Singer of Yisrael (David), finding it only in an ugly act that was performed in the most despicable spot on earth! To that we can only reply with the words of the Godly poet: "Many things have You done, You Eternal, my God; Your wonders and thoughts are for us" (*Tehillim* 40:6; see also *Yevamos* 77a).

Man, however, does not see as God does. Despite all the repulsiveness in Lot's daughters deed, the Inspector of Hearts found in it a positive sign that could serve as a foundation on which to build the world. "[God] said to them, 'You deserved to be destroyed for what you did, but I cannot punish you, because you intended to repopulate My world'" (*Yalkut Shimoni Devarim* 808). Lot's daughters did not do it for base reasons. Following the destruction of Sedom, they thought the whole world had been destroyed and that it was up to them to rebuild it. It was in order to revive the world that they forced themselves to do what was against their nature (see *Ramban* to *Bereshis* 19:32). Their act thus contained a spark of self-sacrifice for the benefit of humanity, a fact the Torah notes by calling them "finds": "your two daughters who are found." Before the daughters of Lot, this was not "found" in the human world. Once this spark glittered in a human soul, it never went out or got lost; rather, it traveled invisibly through generations of degenerate nations, until it reignited in an uncorrupted and pure, gracious and kindly person, namely, Ruth the Mo'aviyah, who had the ability to sacrifice everything to alleviate suffering.

"Two Finds — Ruth the Mo'aviyah and Na'amah the Ammonis"

One may draw a straight line from Lot's elder daughter to her distant descendant Ruth. The former, who said, "Come, let us give our father wine to drink" (*Bereshis* 19:32), repressed her body and soul for the good of the world, performing something which is abhorrent to human nature. Ruth, too, did something that had an aspect of impurity and that went against her character. Yet, it was Bo'az, the most devout man of the generation, who deemed the act as one of kindness: "You have surpassed your first [act of] kindness with your second." This means that the "finding" of Ruth had already been included in the daughters of Lot, as referred to in the above-quoted words of our Sages: " 'Your two daughters who are found' — two finds — Ruth the Mo'aviyah and Na'amah the Ammonis. It had been prophesied concerning her hundreds of years previously, and she was one of the two virtuous doves for whose sake the Holy One, blessed is He, showed pity to two great nations of wicked people, namely Mo'av and Ammon, exhorting Yisrael, 'Do not incite them to war' " (*Bava Kamma* 38; *Yalkut Shimoni Devarim* 808). When this soul descended into the world through the nation of Mo'av, Divine Providence clandestinely masterminded its induction into the Jewish people. This eventuated in the union between the best man in the House of Yisrael and the best dove among the nations, resulting after four generations in the birth of David.

Hence, the entire chain of events that led to the birth of David begins with Lot's daughters, as our Sages stated: "Where did I find him? In Sedom." From the same type of earth that was dug out of the mines of Sedom will sprout forth the last redeemer in the end of days, concerning whom it is prophesied: "A [royal] staff will then be produced from the family line of Yishai, and a sapling will sprout from its roots" (*Yeshayahu* 11:1). This is the power of a good spark that appears to sparkle and disappear, but really gathers strength between exposures and in the end will shine as the sun upon earth and its inhabitants.

"A Descendant That Issued Forth from Elsewhere, and Who Is He? King Mashiach."

Chazal discovered in Sefer Toldos Ha-Adam that the future redemption of mankind is evolving from ancient times through "seed that issues forth from another place." The first source for this is the birth of Shes, concerning whom Scripture states, "She called him Shes (granted), [saying,] 'For God has granted me [an]other offspring, instead of Hevel whom Kayin killed' " (Bereshis 4:25). Chazal explain: "Rav Tanchuma said in the name of Rabbi Shemuel: 'She saw that the child came from "another place," referring to the King Mashiach'" (Bereshis Rabbah 23:7). While we cannot claim to fully comprehend what our Sages meant, this seems to imply that the offspring of Kayin, and that of Shes — who replaced Hevel — constitute two separate sources. Kayin's offspring view everyone else as delimiting their world; that is why Kayin killed Hevel. The Redemption can never sprout from Kayin's seed; another seed is required for such a sapling.

When Shes was born, Chavah recognized that he was that other seed. Inherent in Shes' seed is the trait of seeing others as helpers in building the world. This causes man to restrict himself and make room for others, a characteristic which will serve as the basis for mutuality and the establishment of fairness and justice.

Similarly does the elder daughter of Lot, in her concern over the continuation of the world, speak in the manner of Chavah, not about children [בנים], but about offspring [זרע, lit. seed]: "And we will [thus] produce offspring from our father" (Bereshis 19:34). Noteworthy again is Rav Tanchuma's statement here in the name of Rabbi Shemuel: " 'And we will [thus] produce offspring from our father'; 'a son' is not mentioned, but 'offspring' — this refers to that offspring which comes from 'another place,' referring to the King

Mashiach" (*Bereshis Rabbah* 51:10). Lot's daughter uttered the prophecy that from her action there would emerge not an ordinary son, but offspring that would come from "another place," through which mankind would be redeemed. For the Messianic era would bring a complete victory over the traits that had been ingrained in Kayin's seed, rendering all humankind into "another seed."

"The Most Prominent King"

The hopes associated with offspring that would come "from another place" first began to be realized in David, King of Yisrael, the sweet singer of Yisrael, who is the ancestor of Mashiach, as well as the first to pave the way for him. We have neither the intention nor the competency to describe David's greatness, concerning whom God Himself boasts, "I have found David My servant" (*Tehillim* 89:21). The only guidelines we have are the words of Chazal, who found comparisons between Moshe and David, whom they called, "the most prominent prophet and the most prominent king." Both fought the battles of the Eternal, and David composed five Books [of Psalms] corresponding to the five Books of the Torah (*Midrash Shocher Tov*). That is to say, both are the greatest redeemers and teachers of the people of Yisrael. Futhermore, David is considered as the fourth of our forefathers, as Chazal explain (see *Pesachim* 117b) the verse, "And I have given you a great name, as the names of the prominent ones on earth" (*Shemuel II* 7:9). In the Kabbalah he appears as the fourth leg of the Merkavah (chariot-throne) — that is, he serves as a support to the earthly edifice.

"Ruddy with Fair Eyes"

Seemingly, however, reading in the Bible about David's deeds raises many questions, making it difficult to link his actions to all the notable titles afforded him in the Prophets, Writings, and Oral Torah. Indeed, David had detractors during his lifetime — for example, Shimi ben Gera, concerning whom David himself asserted that "he cursed me

with an explicit [נמרצת] curse" (*Melachim I* 2:8). Chazal state
that the word נמרצת has many connotations, all of them very
caustic. Shimi ben Gera was only one of many, as is evident
from David's own words in *Tehillim* (3:3): "Many say of my
soul, 'There is no release for him from God, Selah.' " Our
Sages explain: Many in Torah, many in stature (i.e., men of
merit and importance), etc. — whatever the word "many"
may imply. All these severely criticized David, making it as if,
God forbid, he had dissociated himself from the God of
Yisrael. David, however, continues, "But You, O Eternal, are
a shield about me." Only the eye of the One Above
ascertained the true essence of David. Even the most
perceptive human eye would likely misjudge him.

Our Sages state that the Prophet Shemuel recoiled at first
because of David's future actions: "Shemuel was frightened
upon seeing that David was ruddy and said, 'He is a spiller
of blood, like Esav.' The Holy One, blessed is He, said to him,
'with fair eyes' (*Shemuel I* 16:12); Esav killed of his own accord,
whereas [David] kills at the behest of the Sanhedrin (*Bereshis
Rabbah* 13:11). While both actions appear similar, there is a
great difference between them: one is murder, and the other,
justice. The difference lies in the motives that cause the act.
Divine truth established that personal motives played no role
at all in any of David's wars. In other words, his personal ego
had no influence on them; he fought them solely for the sake
of law and justice. So does the Prophet attest in the words of
Avigayil: "for my lord fights the wars of the Eternal" (*Shemuel
I* 25:28). David did not fight other wars, those that could not
be categorized as "wars of the Eternal."

Strict law sometimes forced David to perform brutal acts
— for example, against Mo'av, a nation toward whom he
apparently should have felt some kinship, for his ancestress
Ruth came from it. Similarly, he handed over to the Givonim
seven princes from the house of Sha'ul in order to restore
justice. The Midrash (*Bamidbar Rabbah* 8:4) describes how
David tried to appease the Givonim in other ways. Since the
Givonim did not become appeased, however, David stood by

the unaccepted proselytes, administering justice for them against the princes, thereby sanctifying God's name before all nations (see Midrash ibid.). He had to suppress his own ego in all these events. In order to bring about necessary rectifications in the realms of law and justice, he muted his own conscience and acted contrary to his traits and feelings. Thus, he perpetuated the behavior of Lot's daughters and of Ruth, who had found the strength to overcome their emotions.

Justice and Righteousness

David's harsh acts of justice uprooted evil from the world and planted in its stead justice and righteousness. This is explained to us concretely by the words [of Chazal]: "He tested David with sheep and found him to be a good shepherd, as it is stated, 'And He took him from the sheep corrals' (*Tehillim* 78:70) — He restrained the big ones from the small ones; he took the little ones to pasture, so they could eat the soft grass; then he took out the old ones, so they could eat the medium grass; and then he took out the strong ones that would eat the hard grass" (*Shemos Rabbah* 2:2). These words provide a remarkable picture of David's methodology. When he kept the big sheep locked up even as they struggled to get out because they were hungry, he indeed acted cruelly toward them. This cruelty, however, was necessary, in order that the smaller and weaker sheep not be deprived of appropriate pasturage. So did David create a perfect combination of justice and righteousness — justice with the strong and assertive ones; righteousness toward the others. Wherever one sees his justice, there one finds his righteousness.

"Adino the Etzni"

According to our Sages, the Book of Shemuel contains a detailed appraisal of David's character and greatness. Both his apparently contradictory modes of conduct are emphasized there as well, but they are actually one and the same. The passage reads: "These are the names of David's warriors: Yoshev Bashevess, Tachkemoni, Rosh Hashalishi — he is Adino the Etzni" (*Shemuel II* 23:8). Chazal explain that the verse is referring to David himself: Said R. Abbahu: "It means, 'And these are the mighty deeds of David': 'Yoshev Bashevess' means sitting at the session — that is, when he sat in the Yeshivah he did not sit on cushions and quilts, but on the ground. 'Tachkemoni' — Rav said: The Holy One, blessed is He, said to him, 'Since you have humbled yourself, you shall be like Me; I [will] make a decree and you [may] annul it.' 'Rosh Hashalishi' means that you will be chief next to the three Forefathers. 'Adino the Etzni' — When he was sitting and studying the Torah he made himself as pliant as a worm, but when he went out to war he hardened himself like a lance" (*Mo'ed Katan* 16b). Unlike Sha'ul, David knew when to be yielding and when to be rigid (Adin means "delicate"; Etzni means "like wood"). Even when many regarded him as "wooden," the Tester of Hearts recognized that he was Adino, that is, "Ruddy with fair eyes."

The Prophet summarizes David's deeds as follows: "David reigned over all Israel, and David administered justice and righteousness to all his people" (*Shemuel II* 8:15). The Torah states in regard to Avraham: "For I have known him [closely], because he directs his sons and his household after him, that they keep the way of the Eternal by performing righteousness and justice" (*Bereshis* 18:19). Our Forefather Avraham was the first to recognize that justice and righteousness are the way of God, and he implanted them into his family circle. David went further by establishing them as a basis for rule under the Jewish monarchy. He actually proved that it is possible to fix firmly the life of an entire nation on the foundations of justice and righteousness, as the Torah demands. This was his great innovation.

Messianic Mission

In addition to demonstrating to the Jewish people how to correlate and synthesize justice and righteousness, David unveiled new vistas to all humankind. He opened the Book of Psalms with "Fortunate is the man" (*Tehillim* 1:1) — Every single individual who walks in the path of truth is fortunate. Just as the Torah by its very opening, "In the beginning of...creating," enlightened the entire world regarding Creation — as it is stated, "Your opening words illuminate" (*Tehillim* 119:130) — so did David shed light on man's conduct in Creation, with his opening of "Fortunate is the man." It is as if he were saying: "There is a potentiality for happiness in this 'valley of weeping.' " If individuals would adopt the policy of bringing happiness to one another, how fortunate would be all of society!

Psalm 72 speaks about the era when all humanity will attain happiness. In that chapter David prays on behalf of his son Shelomo: "God, endow the king with Your judgments, and Your righteousness to the prince" (*Tehillim* 72:1) — "May the punishments befall me, but treat my son with kindness, so that he will have peace in his days" (Rashi). May the Messianic missions begin in his days and through him. The "Sweet Singer of Yisrael" is outlining here the ideal form of government in ways of justice and peace, founded on the fear of God: "So that they fear You as long as the sun...." May the rule of this perfect king, in "whose days the righteous shall flourish," spread over the entire world, not through wars and conquests, but by all nations realizing that it is the long-awaited government, one of justice and virtue. "May all kings prostrate themselves before him, all nations serve him." Why? Because he will deliver the needy who cries out, and the poor one who has none to help him. He will pity the poor and needy, and save the souls of the needy...and their blood will be precious in their eyes." The blood of the needy will be the most precious and dear blood in his eyes. "May he live, and may [God] give him of the gold of Sh'va." That is to say, the abundance of wealth that will flow to him in the form of gifts from many lands (v. 10) will all be set aside for the poor. "May he live!" When life will be built on these foundations, all of creation will bestow its blessings on man: "There will be an abundance of grain in the land, on the mountaintops, its fruit will rustle like Lebanon." This is in keeping with the Torah's promise: "If you pursue My statutes...I will provide your rains at their [appropriate] time" (*Vayikra* 3–4).

This chapter closes with "The prayers of David, son of Yishai, are ended." When this ideal is realized, and there will be no more individual or communal sorrow, prayers that come from a broken heart will end, and what will remain is a world of song and praise (as per the Radak's commentary). David lifted his heart in prayer for such a Messianic world. The first buds of such a happy life had already been seen in Shelomo's day, but their complete fulfillment is reserved for the days of Mashiach ben David.

This is how David paved the way for the individual and society to the Kingdom of Heaven, where man will attain what he had lacked throughout history, namely, happiness and redemption.

Rabbi Yosef Ze'ev Lipowitz, ztz"l

by Rabbi Dov Katz

Our Sages declared: "The righteous need no monuments; their words are their memorials." The Ga'on, Rabbi Yosef Ze'ev Halevi Lipowitz, *zt"l*, needs neither monuments nor endorsements. The remarkable teachings and lofty ideas which he dispersed with abundance, and which had become engraved upon the hearts of his thousands of students and listeners — a small portion of which have also been published — serve to illuminate his personality and to memorialize his soul.

The late Rabbi Yosef Ze'ev, *zt"l*, was among the few exceptional personalities and lofty souls of his generation. He was an intellectual, a reflective thinker, who never ceased formulating innovative ideas, much like a gushing spring. Whenever and wherever one would meet him, one would find the wellsprings of his heart overflowing with a flood of ideas that were both exhilarating and mesmerizing.

Rabbi Lipowitz expressed himself on every subject: passages of the Torah and Prophets; the various *Aggados* and *Midrashim*; commentaries and homiletic interpretations; works of ethics, inquiry, etc. In all these he evinced expertise and wide-ranging knowledge, always probing the depths, and discovering illuminating, breathtaking pearls and brilliant ideas between the lines.

He also shared his insights regarding world events. He had clear perspectives on history, governments, and politics. He followed current events, commenting on them from a Torah perspective, and pointing to remarkable evidence of

Divine Providence directing the world.

Due to an abundance of inspiration coupled with restlessness, it was difficult for him to remain secluded; hence he grabbed at every opportunity to lecture and teach before all kinds of groups. He never prepared his lectures; his thoughts flowed in a torrent, his ideas spontaneously interweaving themselves, as his emotions gushed forth, beyond his ability to stop or direct them.

R' Yosef's raging forces had already been noticed in youth. He was born in 1889 in Trestina, near Byalistock, Poland. His father, R' Baruch, a Kotzker Chassid, was a learned, affluent businessman. (He died in Tel Aviv.) R' Yosef acquired his early education in his birthplace. His soul, however, was not satisfied by ordinary education, as it yearned for greater things. Thus, upon hearing at the tender age of sixteen about the illustrious Slobodka Yeshivah in Lithuania, he left home for that place of Torah.

His talents in halachic dialectics were immediately recognized, foretelling his future in that area. He distinguished himself by his quick grasp, deep perception, and faultless logic, amazing others with his sharp innovations. He became close to the dean of the Yeshivah, the *Ga'on* Rabbi Moshe Mordechai Epstein, *ztz"l*, joining the group of outstanding students who learned in his inner circle. The *Ga'on* regarded him highly, even asking R' Yosef to substitute for him at his regular Talmud class in Slobodka.

In the fall of 1911, when the *Ga'on* Rabbi Meir Simcha of Dvinsk (the "Ohr Somayach") visited Kovno, R' Yosef Ze'ev was among the outstanding students sent by the heads of the Yeshivah to discuss Torah with him. It happened that the bridge connecting Slobodka and Kovno was washed out, causing R' Yosef Ze'ev to remain an extra few days in Kovno. He took advantage of the situation to draw near unto R' Meir Simcha. It was then that R' Meir Simcha came to know and deeply admire him, as is evidenced from the titles he bestowed on R' Yosef in a letter congratulating him on his wedding: "Wise, young, sharp, proficient scholar, infused with unadulterated Torah and fear of Heaven."

Because R' Yosef Ze'ev was endowed with imagination and fervor, however, he was also captivated by the ethical talks of the Yeshivah's Mashgiach, the *Ga'on* Rabbi Nasan Tzvi Finkel, *zt"l*. The latter's ethical system, based on man's ascendancy and striving toward loftiness and self-perfection, appealed very much to R' Yosef Ze'ev's yearning, emotional soul, causing him to cling to him and to his teachings.

Thus, R' Yosef Ze'ev excelled in both spheres — Halachah and sagacity — simultaneously, becoming recognized as one of the outstanding students of the Slobodka Yeshivah.

In 1912 he married Baila, daughter of a rich merchant from Ritova, Lithuania. She was his faithful companion throughout his life. His father-in-law set him up in a business selling animal hides. Mainly, his wife ran the shop; he would spend just a few hours a day there, devoting the rest of his time to Torah study.

Despite his prosperity, he neither remained indifferent to his surroundings, nor did he rest on his laurels. Shortly after settling down, he and another local young scholar established a *yeshivah* for youngsters where he even taught a daily lesson without pay. Due to his remarkable guidance, he was able to send many of his students to higher *yeshivos*, where they achieved greatness. Following the First World War, the *yeshivah* expanded, due to the assistance of the renowned ethical scholar, Rabbi Shemuel Pondiler, who had then been appointed rabbi in Ritova. R' Yosef Ze'ev found in him a kindred spirit, and worked with him throughout the years to raise the yeshivah's pride and to strengthen the spiritual life of the local inhabitants.

At the end of the year 5684 (before Rosh Hashanah, 1924), R' Yosef Ze'ev liquidated his business and immigrated to the Holy Land. He had always wanted to do that. For years he had saved pennies toward that goal. He settled in Tel Aviv, the first modern Jewish city, quickly becoming part of the new city's life, which was then beginning to take shape, developing into one of its most outstanding religious personalities.

R' Yosef Ze'ev saw his mission in life as disseminating Torah and knowledge in the new community. He first dedicated himself to teaching youth. Soon after arriving he assumed the position of a teacher of Talmud in the upper grades of the Tachkemoni School. He endeared himself to the students, infusing them with a desire to grow in Torah and to continue their studies in *yeshivos*. He also attracted other students from various Torah backgrounds, instructing them privately, succeeding in sending some of them to higher yeshivos as well. He paid particular attention to those who had great potential, and personally accompanied his students to *yeshivos* in Jerusalem. Many went on to eventually become famous rabbis and instructors at yeshivos, serving as a reward for all his efforts.

He later served as a lecturer in the Yeshivah of Tel Aviv, following which he continued to disseminate Torah to the community at large. He dispersed his energies in all directions, speaking, lecturing, and teaching to all kinds of gatherings in the city. For many years he taught the weekly Torah portion and *Ein Ya'akov* daily, between *Minchah* and *Ma'ariv* and following *Ma'ariv*, in one of the Great Synagogue's meeting halls. He devoted his entire Sabbath to lecturing at various city locations. Here is an example from a certain period: Between *Kabbalas Shabbos* and *Ma'ariv*, he spoke at the synagogue in the Neveh Tzedek neighborhood; following the Sabbath evening meal he lectured on the weekly portion at the Great Synagogue; in the morning he would walk to one or another of the city's synagogues — sometimes to one quite far away — to make an appeal on behalf of either a charitable or Torah institution, or to strengthen Jewish values, depending on his given assignment; in the afternoon he taught Midrash in the main hall of the Great Synagogue; and between *Minchah* and

Ma'ariv he delivered special lectures to *Sephardim*. On *Motza'ei Shabbos* as well, he would teach special classes to particular groups, study circles, etc. Besides all these activities, he was in great demand and served as main speaker at conferences, meetings, celebrations, and parties whenever possible. He was Tel Aviv's uncrowned "City Preacher."

The main content of his speeches was based on the foundations of *Mussar* (ethical thought) that he had received from his mentors, which encompassed all areas of life and Jewish values. He believed this system to be closest to the spirit of the Torah. Scholars of ethical thought arrive at concepts from the text or aphorism. After delving into the meaning of the text or statement, they are able to uncover its concealed meaning. Thus, they do not create an idea, but rather bring forth the Torah's intent.

To top it all off, he would then add his original thoughts, using his unique style and genial manner. He would use stories, parables, and flowery language, mixed occasionally with humor. He was a silver-tongued orator who was also blessed with the ability to make his words relevant and infused with life, thus rendering them enlightening and cheerful.

To alleviate their subsistence, his wife turned part of their home into a guest house and a special dining room for students of the Torah. Thus, their home became a meeting place for scholars. Mostly Torah personalities dined at their table, causing the walls of their home to constantly echo with the sounds of Torah and ethical dialectics led by the host himself. This house became known in Tel Aviv as a holy retreat for scholars and lofty personalities, where many came to satisfy their spiritual thirst.

Thanks to all these activities of R' Yosef Ze'ev, he became renowned in Tel Aviv and beyond as a thinker, wise in the fear of Hashem, polite, and well-mannered, which gained him acceptance among all the diverse circles of society. Even authors and persons of great accomplishment came to meet with him in order to bask in the light of his teaching and to invigorate themselves through his original insights.

R' Yosef Ze'ev was conspicuous also because of his fine personality traits. Especially noteworthy were his humility and modesty. He always conducted himself unpretentiously, without a trace of haughtiness or the pursuit of honor. Despite his participation in numerous activities and appearances, he did not request that they be publicized, the result being that his name rarely appeared in announcements.

R' Yosef Ze'ev also excelled in the virtue of loving-kindness. In his book on *Megillas Ruth*, he is profuse in praising this attribute, using such phrases as: "The world is built on kindness"; "Kindness is the axis around which the entire Torah revolves"; "One is gauged by one's kindness"; "One's spirituality may be discerned by this virtue, for it raises one above egoism"; "Wisdom, strength, and wealth that are not galvanized by the spirit of kindness are not ends in themselves, but are in fact detrimental"; "Hashem's desire from creation was kindness, justice, and righteousness."

He practiced what he preached. He sought out acts of kindness and rejoiced at every opportunity to do favors. Needless to say, he was most careful to refrain from hurting anyone. He received everyone cordially, with pleasant and heartfelt words. His home was open to all, and no one ever left it empty-handed. He loaned money to Torah scholars and others who were needy, even borrowing to do so, when necessary. He would not hesitate to use his friendship with Tel Aviv officials, or his own good name, to good influence. He thus assisted many morally, or financially — for example, through support, employment, appointment, and the like. Similarly, he assisted the many who turned to him for teaching or speaking material.

About seven years before his passing, he developed heart trouble. Doctors then instructed him to refrain from public speaking and to limit his conversation. He stopped appearing in public, but continued studying and developing new thoughts, sharing these with all who came to visit him or who were close to him. Many Torah personalities and moralists took this opportunity to visit him.

It was during that period that R' Yosef Ze'ev found time to organize some of his thoughts on *Megillas Ruth*. He published them as a commentary on that Megillah, titled *Nachalas Yosef*. It is through this book that one may get a glimpse of some of his bright light and of the hidden treasures that were his thoughts and ideas. Here is revealed his ability to unravel the profundity and concealed meanings of the statements of *Chazal*, to plumb to the depths of the powers of the human soul, and to present clear pictures of life's dreams and experiences. Here is also exposed the nature of the author's lofty personality, as well as his resplendent, all-embracing, delightful worldview.

To perpetuate his noteworthy ideas, during his last years his devotees recorded his lectures. Thanks to this, it was possible to edit, translate, and publish his works on the Torah.

Despite his increasing weakness of the last few years, R' Yosef Ze'ev sat diligently over his books until his last day, his mouth continuing to emit pearls of Torah and wisdom. He quietly returned his soul to his Maker on the 8th of Nisan 5722 (12 April 1962). Due to the fact that not many received the sad news in time, very few were able to pay him his last respects. May his name be perpetuated through his work.

A Letter of Congratulations to the Author by the Ga'on, the "Ohr Somayach"

B"H
Friday, Eve of the Sabbath of *"Ben Poras Yosef"*...

From the depths of my heart I congratulate the learned young scholar, whose learning is sharp and erudite, and who is awash in Torah and pure fear of God, Rabbi Yosef Ze'ev Halevi Lipowitz, and his extolled bride, on their wedding.

May Hashem grant them much blessing, happiness, and wealth. May they build a house in Israel and succeed, flourish as a vine ... May their parents be blessed, and may they merit seeing joy and goodness from them and their progeny. This is the wish and blessing of one who esteems the Torah and those who study it.

Meir Simcha Hakohen of Dvinsk